Standards-Based Activities With Scoring Rubrics:

Middle & High School English

Volume 1

Performance-Based Portfolios

Jacqueline Glasgow, Editor

EYE ON EDUCATION
6 DEPOT WAY WEST, SUITE 106
LARCHMONT, NY 10538
(914) 833–0551
(914) 833–0761 fax
www.eyeoneducation.com

Library of Congress Cataloging-in-Publication Data

Standards-based activities with scoring rubrics : middle and high school English / [edited by] Jacqueline Glasgow.
     p. cm.
Includes bibliographical references.
Contents: v. 1. Performance-based portfolios. — v. 2. Performance-based projects.
ISBN 1-930556-28-4 (v. 1) — ISBN 1-930556-29-2 (v. 2)
    1. English language—United States—Examinations. 2. Academic achievement—United States—Evaluation. 3. English language—Study and teaching (Secondary)—Standards—United States. I. Glasgow, Jacqueline, 1941–

LB1631.5 .S78 2002
428'.0074—dc21

10 9 8 7 6 5 4 3 2 1

2001051221

Editorial and production services provided by
Richard H. Adin Freelance Editorial Services
52 Oakwood Blvd., Poughkeepsie, NY 12603-4112
(845-471-3566)

CONTRIBUTORS

Jacqueline Glasgow, Ph.D.
Associate Professor of English
Education
Ohio University, Athens

Ruth McClain, Teacher
Paint Valley High School
Chillicothe, Ohio

Tom Flynn, Ph.D.
Associate Professor of English
Ohio University, Eastern

Margie Bush, Teacher
Shawnee High School
Lima, Ohio

Nanci Bush, Teacher
Solon High School
Solon, Ohio

Susan Malaska, Teacher
Shelby High School
Shelby, Ohio

Janie Reinart
English/Language Arts Consultant
S. Russell, Ohio

Linda Rice, Teacher
Lakeview High School
Cortland, Ohio

Joyce Rowland, Teacher
Bristol High School
Bristolville, Ohio

Colleen Ruggieri, Teacher
Boardman High School
Youngstown, Ohio

Carolyn Suttles, Teacher
Bristol High School
Bristolville , Ohio

Acknowledgments

Many thanks to the Ohio Department of Education (ODE) for funding the project that has resulted in two volumes of best practice performance-based assessments for Middle School and High School English teachers. We are indebted to Dr. J. Daniel Good, Director of the Center for Curriculum and Assessment at ODE, and Dr. Kent Minor, Assistant Director of Professional Development and Licensure at ODE, for their confidence in the Ohio Council of Teachers of English to produce this work. We thank Bob Taft, Governor of Ohio, and Dr. Susan Tave Zelman, Ohio Superintendent of Public Instruction, for privileging the research and development of performance-based assessment practices.

This work could not have been completed without the strong support of the Executive Board of the Ohio Council of Teachers of English and Language Arts (OCTELA). OCTELA members submitted entries, gathered at weekend retreats, and volunteered their services in drafting, revising, and editing the manuscript as it progressed. Through team effort, our understanding of performance-based assessments has emerged into the two volumes in your hands today.

Many thanks to Bob Sickles and the staff at Eye on Education for their support in making these publications the best possible. I'd also like to thank the external reviewers Helen Dale, Joan Heiss, Pat Rooney, Myra Vinson, and Jennifer Watson.

Jacqueline Glasgow

Table of Contents

Also Available from EYE ON EDUCATION

Standards-Based Activities with Scoring Rubrics:
Middle and High School English
Volume 2, Performance-Based Projects
Edited by Jacqueline Glasgow

Socratic Seminars & Literature Circles
for Middle and High School English
Victor and Marc Moeller

High School English Teacher's
Guide to Active Learning
Victor and Marc Moeller

Middle School English Teacher's
Guide to Active Learning
Victor and Marc Moeller

An English Teacher's Guide to Performance Tasks
and Rubrics: High School
Amy Benjamin

An English Teacher's Guide to Performance Tasks
and Rubrics: Middle School
Amy Benjamin

Writing in the Content Areas
Amy Benjamin

Teaching English in the Block
Strzepek, Newton, and Walker

Developing Parent and Community
Understanding of Performance-Based Assessment
Kathryn Alvestad

Constructivist Strategies:
Meeting Standards and Engaging Adolescent Minds
Foote, Vermette, and Battaglia

Performance Standards and Authentic Learning
Allan A. Glatthorn

Part I

Standards-Based Assessment

1

OVERVIEW

In this era of state proficiencies and high-stakes testing, the burdens of preparing students for standardized assessments has, at times, seemed to rob teachers of their willingness to "teach on the edge." This book presents a rich array of performance-based and standards-based activities with ready-made scoring tools designed to ensure accountability and celebrate the joy of learning simultaneously. By aligning standards, performance tasks (i.e., the activities found throughout this book), and assessments according to Glatthorn's model of authentic learning and performance assessment (Figure 1.1), teachers can demonstrate that teaching on the edge, where joy, interaction, and innovation are the heart of the classroom, not only "measures up to," but can indeed surpass (and be a whole lot more fun than) "teaching to the test."

This is a book written by teachers for teachers. It is not prescriptive; rather, it is informational and allows the individual district and teacher the freedom to accept, reject, and modify any of the suggestions. In fact, we hope that teachers will see the many opportunities provided for innovative and creative teaching and assessment that recognizes the interrelationship of curriculum and assessment presented in this book. We have included three types of performance assessments: (1) a single piece of writing, (2) portfolio collections (literary and personal), and (3) multimedia assessments (dramatic, multimedia, oral, and museum). The purpose of this book is to enhance the quality of language learning in secondary English classrooms that is anchored in Glatthorn's Model of Authentic Learning, NCTE/IRA Standards for Language Arts Programs, and Falk's Using Standards and Assessment to Learn.

Authentic Learning Occurs in a Standards-Based Curriculum for English Language Arts

Glatthorn suggests that authentic learning is more likely to occur if the required curriculum is "derived from quality standards" (1999, p. 28). The standards published by the National Council of Teachers of English and the International Reading Association (NCTE/IRA) list 12 quality standards to guide curriculum for English Language Arts. The vision guiding these standards is that all students must have the opportunities and resources to develop the language skills they need to pursue life goals and to participate fully as informed, productive members of society. The standards provide a foundation for curriculum

Figure 1.1 Glatthorn's Model of Authentic Learning and Assessment

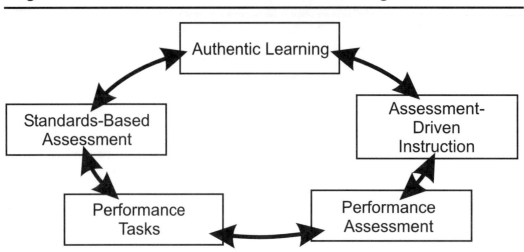

development. Standards for the English Language Arts (SELA) tells us that in the classroom we will find:

- students who are playing the roles of readers and writers, discovering how to shape their experience and to connect their experience to text;
- evidence of public audiences, classroom audiences, and personal audiences playing the roles of reader and responder to student work;
- subject matter, whether imaginary, public/civic, or academic and informational;
- different tools (computers, telephones, calculators, faxes) and editing groups;
- various texts both literary and nonliterary for reading, hearing, and viewing;
- language reference books on the structure of grammar (phonology, morphology, syntax) and text; and
- evidence of cognitive and metacognitive development in drafts from editing, discussion, and response groups, including learning logs, outlines, notes, and other forms (Myers and Spalding 1997, p. ix).

Literate people today must be effective communicators, critical thinkers, creative problem solvers, and lifelong learners. A curriculum built on these standards will encourage students to read a wide variety of print and nonprint texts, seek answers to meaningful questions, and appreciate the power and diversity of language as participating members of literacy communities. A curriculum built on these standards will enable students to develop their abilities in speaking, listening, reading, writing, viewing, and visual representation.

Authentic Learning Occurs if Based on a Meaningful Performance Task

According to Glatthorn, authentic learning is more likely to occur when students are engaged in a meaningful performance task. A performance task is "a complex open-ended problem posed for the student to solve as a means of demonstrating mastery" (Glatthorn 1999, p. 18). Marzano and Kendall (1996) identify the following characteristics of a performance task:

- requires knowledge to be applied to a specific situation
- provides necessary guidance and information to complete the task;
- specifies learning context (independent, pairs, small groups);
- specifies how students will demonstrate their findings or solution.

Once the performance tasks are identified, then the unit of instruction can be developed so that the students can do well when the assessment is made. Of course, the unit should be based on the approved curriculum guide for the school district. Performance tasks can be developed to prepare students for state performance assessments or to enrich the English Language Arts curriculum. Stiggins (1997) stresses that well-designed performance assessments are a highly effective teaching tool, significantly fostering student learning.

Authentic Learning Occurs Through Authentic Assessment

If we regard learning as a process of actively constructing meaning, rather than an accumulation of skills, then assessment tools must reflect our beliefs. Although traditional assessments, such as asking students to respond to writing prompts, are useful for preparing them to take proficiency tests, we encourage teachers to move toward more authentic assessment and evaluation. We want students to think, question, research, write, and share the meaning they have constructed.

Authentic assessment is geared toward methods that correspond as closely as possible to real-world experience. It was originally developed in the arts and apprenticeship systems, where assessment has always been based on performance. The instructor observes the student in the process of working on something real, provides feedback, monitors the student's use of feedback, and adjusts instruction and evaluation accordingly. Authentic assessment takes this principle of evaluating real work into all areas of the curriculum.

The rubric is one authentic assessment tool that is designed to simulate real-life activity where students are engaged in solving real-life problems. It is a formative type of assessment because the assessment rubric is available to students at the beginning of instruction serving as a learning tool. As students work toward meeting the expectations specified in the rubric, it becomes an ongoing part of the whole teaching and learning process. Students themselves can be involved in the assessment process using the rubric for both peer and self-assessment. As students become familiar with rubrics, they can assist in the rubric design process. This involvement empowers the students and, as a result, their learning becomes more focused and self-directed. Authentic assessment, therefore, blurs the lines between teaching, learning, and assessment. The advantages of using rubrics in assessment are that they:

- ◆ allow assessment to be more objective and consistent
- ◆ focus the teacher to clarify her/his criteria in specific terms
- ◆ clearly show the student how their work will be evaluated and what is expected
- ◆ promote student awareness of the criteria to use in assessing peer performance
- ◆ provide useful feedback regarding the effectiveness of the instruction
- ◆ provide benchmarks against which to measure and document progress

Rubrics can be created in a variety of forms and levels of complexity. However, they all contain common features that:

- ◆ focus on measuring a goal, standard, or benchmark (performance, behavior, or quality),
- ◆ provide a list of criteria for the project (assignment), and
- ◆ contain specific performance characteristics arranged in levels indicating the degree to which a standard has been met.

According to Starr (2000), a good rubric should:

- ◆ address all relevant content and performance objectives;
- ◆ define standards and help students achieve them by providing criteria with which they can evaluate their own work;
- ◆ be easy to understand and use;
- ◆ be applicable to a variety of tasks;
- ◆ provide all students with an opportunity to succeed at some level;
- ◆ yield consistent results, even when administered by different scorers.

The main drawback to using rubrics for assessment is that students want rubrics for everything they learn! (Adapted from Rubrics for Web Lessons: http://edweb.sdsu.edu/webquest/rubrics/weblessons.htm.)

Standards-Based Assessment Activities and Scoring Rubrics

Based on the above theory and research, these two volumes contain a variety of standards-based and performance-based assessments with scoring rubrics. Also included are excellent models of student work to stimulate the imagination and demonstrate creative responses to the assessments. See Volume 1 for Traditional and Portfolio Assessments and Volume 2 for Performance-Based Project Assessments.

Traditional Assessment: Essays and Other Single Pieces of Writing (Volume 1)

Students read and write for specific purposes and to learn basic writing formats and conventions. Expository writing provides the best opportunity to directly teach the most important foundations of good writing: the development of coherence, logic, and ideas within the structural confines of the paragraph and the essay while supporting with evidence those claims that writers wish to make. If the essay is written as a one-shot event, the product is valued over the writing process. If the essay has traveled through peer editing and multiple drafting, the writing process has been observed and revision has been valued. For the teacher, this assessment provides a quick reference for remediation and intervention. In volume one of this book, prompts, scoring rubrics, and student samples are provided to help students meet the standards for the narrative, expository, and persuasive modes of writing found on many proficiency exams.

Personal and Literary Portfolio Collections (Volume 1)

These assessments consist of a collection of work, from writing folders to scrapbooks to mandated collections of work that showcase the student as a learner. Departing from the traditional writing portfolio that results in key artifacts from an entire year to show growth and development, these various types of portfolios fulfill a variety of purposes. Most of the portfolios in this book represent thematic units and therefore document the student's literacy by integrating reading, writing, art, music, technology, and other content areas. Portfolio assessments not only show the students' critical judgments and collaborative processes, but they also provide documentation of meeting district, state, and national standards. In volume one of this book, there are ideas for portfolios comprised of responses to literary collections such as cyber buddy journals, poetry notebooks, literature circles, and scrapbooks. The personal portfolio collections include an archaeological dig, "I Search Paper," sketch books and other types of journals.

Performance-Based Project Assessments (Volume 2)

These performance-based project assessments encourage teachers to use the most progressive means possible for assessing a student's literacy performance. The activities included in this assessment ask students to demonstrate literacy through performance and presentations (mimes, dance); visual arts (music, photographs, sketches, cartoons); media literacy; multimedia performances; and technology projects in HyperStudio, PowerPoint, and/or Web pages.

These projects fulfill the performance objectives for composition, listening/ visual literacy, oral communication, and reading mandated in the NCTE/IRA Standards. Teachers and students who work with these kinds of performance activities are engaged in active responses that recognize and develop individual talents, thinking strategies, and modes of expression. Volume two of this book, provides examples of performance assessments through drama, multimedia projects, oral performances, and museums, as well as appropriate assessment rubrics.

Bibliography

Falk, B. (2000). *The heart of the matter: Using standards and assessment to learn.* Portsmouth, NH: Heinemann.

Farell, E. (1996). *Standards for the English language arts.* Urbana, IL: National Council of Teachers of English/International Reading Association.

Glatthorn, A. A. (1999). *Performance standards authentic learning.* Larchmont, NY: Eye on Education.

Marzano, R.J., & Kendall, J.S. (1996). *A comprehensive guide to designing standards-based districts, schools, and classrooms.* Alexandria, VA: Association for Supervision and Curriculum Development.

Myers, M., & Spalding, E. (1997). *Standards exemplar series: Assessing student performance grades 9-12.* Urbana, IL: National Council of Teachers of English.

Pickett, N., & Dodge, B. (June 20, 2001). Rubrics for Web lessons [Online]. Available: http://edweb.sdsu.edu/webquest/rubrics/weblessons.htm.

Standards for the English language arts (1996). Urbana, IL: National Council of Teachers of English/International Reading Association.

Starr, L. (2000). *A good rubric.* Education World. Found at: http://education-world.com/a-curr/curr248.htm.

Stiggins, R. J. (1997). *Student-centered classroom assessment (2nd ed.).* Columbus, OH: Merrill.

2

ASSESSING A SINGLE PIECE OF WRITING

Jacqueline Glasgow

We are all apprentices in a craft where no one ever becomes a master.

Ernest Hemingway

Understanding the purpose in writing is basic to deciding how to use writing in the English classroom. When we know the purpose, we then know what to assess. When the purpose is to take accurate notes for a science project, then the notes can be assessed for selectivity and accuracy. When the purpose is to write a letter to the editor of the local newspaper, the letter can be assessed according to whether it is intended to be informative or persuasive. We can teach students to identify the characteristics of writing that they do for diverse reasons. They will see many overlaps, but they will also see some features that are emphasized in *persuasion*, perhaps, that are not important in a *personal narrative*. The need for textual references in *interpretation* is not a hallmark of *reflection*. An essay may well combine interpretive and reflective elements; the criteria for assessing the essay may be adjusted accordingly. The emphasis on writing types is not to limit the teacher or student working within these types as strict frameworks, but to use them as a guide to helping students see that different uses of writing require different emphases. It is easier to work from specific types than to begin with the hybrids that make up many of our day-to-day uses of writing. We provide performance tasks and assessment rubrics for expressive, informative, persuasive, and literary assessments of writing.

NCTE/IRA Standards

In these assessments, students will:

♦ respond to prompts that require expressive, informative, persuasive and literary or aesthetic types of writing. In doing so, students adjust their use of spoken, written, and visual language to communicate effectively with a variety of audiences and for different purposes (NCTE/IRA Standard #4); they will employ a wide range of strategies as they write and use different writing process elements appropriately to communicate with different audiences for a variety of purposes (NCTE/IRA Standard #5); and students will apply knowledge of language structure, language conventions, media techniques, figurative language, and genre to create, critique, and discuss print and nonprint texts (NCTE/IRA Standard #6).

Performance Tasks for Assessing a Single Piece of Writing

We know we have the potential for creating a great many purposes for writing, each of which leads to a piece with identifiable features. It is these features that distinguish what some call *discourse types* or *writing types*. In *A Measure of Success: From Assignment to Assessment in English Language Arts* (1996), Claggett refers to them as *writing types*. She suggests that we can teach students to be thinking or *transactive* writers by involving them in learning to articulate their purposes for writing and then showing them how different purposes require different approaches. With a clear sense of audience and purpose, and an understanding of the features that characterize writing for different purposes, students can engage in productive writing response groups and learn the art of true revision. The resulting pieces can be evaluated by both teachers and students based on a common understanding of what constitutes an effective piece of a particular type of writing.

Claggett differentiates between a *genre* and a *writing type* that is distinguished by author purpose rather than by the stylistic or formal features of a genre. Her model depicting four global writing types combines James Britton's (1977) ideas with Louise Rosenblatt's (1995) aesthetic/efferent continuum. (See Figure 2.1 Global Writing Types). In Britton's model, expressive writing is the groundwork that gives rise to both transactional (writing for purposes of communicating specific information) and poetic writing (writing for aesthetic purposes). Rosenblatt's model, also built on the idea of writer purpose, shows aesthetic and efferent purposes at the extremes, but indicates that purpose is a matter of emphasis rather than exclusion. By helping students identify the naturally occurring features of these four global writing types, we are also teaching students to be able to identify the features that will form the bases for their own, their peers', and their teachers' evaluations of their work.

Figure 2.1 Global Writing Types

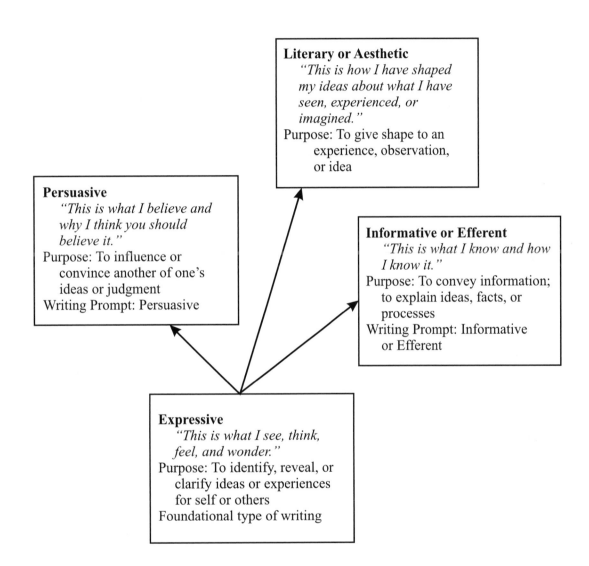

Literary or Aesthetic
"This is how I have shaped my ideas about what I have seen, experienced, or imagined."
Purpose: To give shape to an experience, observation, or idea

Persuasive
"This is what I believe and why I think you should believe it."
Purpose: To influence or convince another of one's ideas or judgment
Writing Prompt: Persuasive

Informative or Efferent
"This is what I know and how I know it."
Purpose: To convey information; to explain ideas, facts, or processes
Writing Prompt: Informative or Efferent

Expressive
"This is what I see, think, feel, and wonder."
Purpose: To identify, reveal, or clarify ideas or experiences for self or others
Foundational type of writing

Reprinted from A Measure of Success: From Assignment to Assessment in English Language Arts by Fran Claggett. Copyright ©1996 by Mary Frances Claggett. Published by Heinemann, a division of Reed Elsevier, Inc., Portsmouth, NH. Used by permission of the publisher.

This model is designed to encompass the variety of purposes for which we write. It acknowledges that expressive writing establishes a foundation for all the other types.

Expressive Writing:
"This is what I see, think, feel, and wonder."

Expressive writing deals with thoughts, ideas, observations, and feelings, which may take the form of diary or journal entries, as well as pieces like personal letters or reflective pieces that might be read by friends. It is the primary means by which emergent writers develop fluency, discover and clarify what they think, and engage in reflection. The purposes for writing expressive pieces vary widely. These purposes may be descriptive, thoughtful, or exploratory in nature and may incorporate narrative strategies such as action, dialogue, and chronological sequencing. Writing to learn new concepts and ideas is the purpose of learning logs. When composed and shaped for an audience beyond that of close friends, such writing moves into the aesthetic realm and may emerge as story, autobiography, poem, or essay. Teachers facilitate writing development when they assign expressive writing through journals, reading response logs, and writer's notebooks, and when they give students the responsibility for choosing their own topics for writing (Claggett, 64).

Assessing Expressive Writing

How should one assess expressive writing? Certainly journals and reading logs should never be graded for the conventions of writing, but reader response comments are usually highly regarded and welcomed by students. This is a place to respond positively and informally by writing notes to the student either in the margins or, if we do not wish to intrude permanently on the student's writing, on Post-its. If through writing workshops, students are asked to polish a piece of expressive writing, then an assessment rubric might be appropriate. See *Assessment Rubric for Expressive Writing Essay* and *Exemplary Student Essay for Expressive Writing*, on page 14.

Assessment Rubric for Expressive Writing Essay

Score	Meaning (clarity, focus, fluency)	Structure (organization, flow)	Language (grammar, dialect, word choice)	Format (Creativity)
10	The piece has a clear focus, fluent writing with clearly developed thoughts and details; shows evidence of reflection	The ideas are clearly organized, with the ideas flowing smoothly in a logical progression	The language is vivid, imaginative, with correct and colorful word choice and description using sensory language	Creative, original expressive ideas in the best format for the message; strong voice present
8–9	The piece makes a point, but lacks either a clear focus or elaboration of details	The organization is coherent and conveys the message logically	Efficient use of language, but needs variety of sentence length and style	Conventional view, but aesthetically pleasing; some awareness of audience; weak voice
6–7	The piece lacks a sustained focus as a result of extraneous or loosely-related details	A clear, but simple organizational structure is apparent, although the focus may shift or the paper may lack coherency	Insufficient variety of sentences and lacks sophistication of language usage	Nothing new or original. Surface-level treatment of the topic; a personal style or voice is not identifiable
3–5	Although there is very little development of ideas, a few reasons or examples are evident	There is scant evidence of a controlling structure	Word choices are limited; there are errors in sentence structure.	Blah! Same old, same old! No individual voice emerges
0–2	There is little supporting detail or examples to create meaning	Development of ideas is inconsistent, inadequate, or illogical.	Word choices are inappropriate. There are many incorrect sentences.	YAWN! No evidence of individual voice

Exemplary Student Essay for Expressive Writing

Niki Watkins, Student
Nicole McBurney, Teacher
Brookfield High School
Expressive—No Prompt Given

The Life of my Adidas Pullover Jacket

Umm, hello. Don't mind me. I'm rather quite shy. I usually don't say much. But today, I think I'll let the world know what it is like to be Niki Watkins's pullover jacket.

Well, I'm an orange and blue, hooded, Adidas pullover jacket. I usually don't get worn a lot, or for a very long period of time when she actually puts me on. I just hang on this white, plastic hanger, next to her other jackets and clothes. But today, she pulled me off of my hanger and threw me onto her bed. (I really hate when she tosses me around like that. I have a slight case of motion sickness.)

Oh…uh…ouch…careful. Okay, she put me on. She must be ready to leave. Ow! She put her book bag on her back. That heavy thing smothers me. What does she carry in that thing anyway? Now, we're descending down the steps… going through the kitchen. She is opening the door. Finally, we're outside. Yuck, it's raining, and windy, and cold. I hate this weather. Now I'm going to get all wet.

We're officially on our way to school. I have a feeling this is going to be a very exciting day. Can't she walk any faster? I'm getting soaked! We've arrived at her friend's house. I guess she is getting a ride to school today. Alright, we're getting into a car. What is she doing? She's beating my sleeves! Just leave the water there, Niki. It's not going to dry! You know, I don't think she realizes how much she hurts me sometimes. Now we're out of the car and back into the rain. Any minute and we'll be in the building.

Thank God! We're in the school. Now I don't have to worry about getting wet anymore. What's that smell? Oh, I remember now. We're on the Junior High hallway. It always smells on this floor. We're now headed up a flight of stairs… going down a long hallway… turning a corner. Good, we're at her locker.

Relief! She took that thing off her back. Now I can breathe. Oh no, here it comes. Please, be gentle. She took me off. And now, I'm on a little hook in a small, enclosed space. Hey, watch it! Something was just shoved into me.

Oh, it's only her friend's jacket. Now it's dark, really dark. I'm afraid of the dark. The other jacket keeps trying to comfort me, but he's not helping. When is Niki coming back?

~Approx. 6 hours and 45 minutes later...~

You're back! You're back! She's back! Oh, I love you, I love you, I love you! Get me out of here! This other jacket is a freak! Yes, finally, I'm free! I'm on Niki again- and so is that stupid book bag, heavier than ever. I can't wait to go home. I'm so exhausted.

The ride home was quiet. I was enjoying the freedom of being out of her locker. And I got some fresh air, too. It stopped raining, so I didn't have to worry about getting wet again. I'm back on my hanger, just in case you were wondering. You know, being a jacket isn't all it's cracked up to be. But I do have to be thankful that I'm not a sock, or even a shoe. I hear them complain all day. It gives me a hoodache. But, now I'm tired. I had a long day. I hope you got some idea what it's like to be a jacket. Did I do my job? I hope so. And hey, come visit me sometime. Talk to me. (I get lonely a lot.) And I promise, I'll be a good listener. Well, until I see you again, goodnight.

Informative or Efferent Writing: *"This is what I know and how I know it."*

Informative writing presents what a writer knows about a subject in a way that communicates that knowledge effectively to a reader. It takes into account the needs of readers by putting the information into an appropriate context—orienting the reader, giving appropriate examples, disclosing background, and citing sources of information. Successful informative writers explain their ideas and elaborate information with sufficient detail to provide the reader with a clear understanding of the subject.

Informative writing provides readers with information about a topic rather than persuading them to share a point of view or take action. It focuses on a topic or subject rather than on the writer's private experience or attitude toward the subject. On the other hand, effective informative writing may use point of view and personal anecdote to reveal the writer as a knowledgeable source of information with a commitment to sharing this information with others. In its highly crafted form, informational writing encompasses both aesthetic and efferent purposes. The expository mode of writing is the vehicle for conveying informative writing.

Writing Prompts that Require Informational or Expository Responses

The student will compose an informational (expository) paper that, depending on the selected prompt, defines ideas, describes reasons, explores a problem and its solutions, analyzes cause and effect, classifies, or illustrates.

Expository Prompt One

What person or event has had a significant impact on your life? Describe in detail the person's influence on you, or what happened, and how your life has changed as a result.

Expository Prompt Two

What irritates you the most? Make certain to define the problem and provide specific examples that explain why it bothers you. Propose a positive solution to the problem.

Expository Prompt Three

What is the most important thing a student should know before beginning high school.

Expository Prompt Four

Imagine that you are granted three wishes. State what they are, explain why you chose them, and how they will affect your life.

Assessing Informative Writing

Students can help build a rubric for assessing informative writing once they understand the nature of this kind of writing. The characteristics that can be assessed are focus and coherence, presentation and elaboration, and style. Since this kind of writing has a specific audience, the use of conventions may also be the basis for a separate score. See *Assessment Rubric for Expository Writing* that is based on the scoring rubric for the ninth-grade proficiency test by the Ohio Department of Education. See also the *Exemplary Student Essay for Expository Writing* on page 18.

Assessment Rubric for Expository Writing

	Exemplary 4 Points	*Very Good 3 Points*	*Satisfactory 2 Points*	*Limited 1 Point*
Meaning (clarity, focus, topic connection)	The piece has a clear focus, connects to the topic well and has rich supporting ideas, reasons, or examples; written from experience	The piece is relevant to the topic with adequate supporting ideas or examples and development may be uneven	The piece demonstrates an awareness of the topic; some supporting ideas or example are included but are not developed	The piece is only slightly related to the topic, offering few supporting ideas or examples
Structure (organization, flow)	Excellent beginning, middle, and conclusion; strong transitions; strong logical progression and flow of ideas	Good introduction, placement of details, and ending. Logical order is apparent, although some lapses occur.	An organizational pattern has been attempted	The piece exhibits little or no evidence of an organizational pattern
Language (imagery, dialect, word choice)	The writing demonstrates a mature command of language with strong verbs, specific, concrete nouns and imagery	The writing demonstrates a good command of language and word choice is generally adequate and precise	The writing demonstrates a limited command of language; vocabulary is adequate, but limited, predictable, and occasionally vague	Limited or inappropriate vocabulary obscures meaning
Voice	The piece exhibits a strong, honest, natural voice and style	The piece exhibits a clear personal style and voice	The piece exhibits an emerging style and voice	No individual style or voice evident
Conventions	With few exceptions, the paper follows the conventions of punctuation, capitalization, and spelling	The conventions of punctuation, capitalization, and spelling are generally followed	Some knowledge of conventions of punctuation and capitalization is demonstrated. With few exceptions, commonly used words are spelled correctly	Frequent and blatant errors occur in punctuation, capitalization and commonly used words are frequently misspelled

Exemplary Student Essay for Expository Writing

Amy Spencer
Rita Elavsky, Teacher
Cuyahoga Falls High School

Expository Prompt One—A Person that Changed Your Life

I was first introduced to the group known as Kids On Broadway (K.O.B.) in 1991. It was the perfect place for young singers and actors such as my sister and me. For the next five years after our successful auditions, we were part of this group. We all sang for road shows at the IX Center, the malls all around the areas, and several dozen other places in Ohio. At Bedford High School, we performed at least three major musicals a year with the traditional holiday festival around Christmas. It was during my hours with K.O.B. that I met and befriended Mr. Duane Mathias.

Mr. Mathias was the director of the music/singing half of the whole of Kids On Broadway (Ruth Kerr ran the drama/acting half). Mr. Mathias became like a musical mentor to me and to almost everyone else in the group. His humor and style of piano playing always kept us laughing and encouraged throughout each rehearsal. When it was the opening night of a show, he gave us a morale-enhancing lecture in the green room. Everyone was then willing to give their all for that night, and "fight to the death", if you will. Some of the musicals included Music Man, Annie Get Your Gun, The Mikado, Joseph and the Amazing Technicolor Dream Coat, and The Pirates of Penzance (these are probably the most well-known of the dozens we performed).

Being a director with the opera as well as K.O.B., Mr. Mathias could train us to sing better than we thought possible. Thus, my vocal abilities took several leaps upward during those five years. I also overcame my stage fright to a certain degree with his help. When given the opportunity, and the interest, I had the courage to audition for all of the solos that I've come across (in or out of Kids On Broadway). After performing the solos that I received, I was blessed by the number of people, whom I've never met before, who told me how wonderfully I did, or what a beautiful voice I have. I've also auditioned for the musical and fall play of the two years I've been in high school. I received a major role in both of the plays (Nun of Your Business, and The Bad Seed) and was a chorus member of both musicals (42nd Street, and State

Fair). Continuing my love for music, at the end of my sophomore year, I auditioned for the well-known Show Choir, Melodymen & the Melodettes (M& Ms) and have become a member.

Coming back to after my fifth year of Kids On Broadway, I signed up for private piano lessons with Mr. Mathias. I was taught by him for about two years and developed a deeper love for the piano. I haven't had lessons since then, but I still have the same passion for it. I've even written some of the music that I play often.

Mr. Mathias was a great inspiration for me; he taught me to have fun with music, so I do. He used to work at the middle school that I went to, but Mr. Robert Elkins assumed the position. Mr. Elkins once said that he'd met Mr. Mathias on a few occasions, commenting that he seemed like a "really nice guy." Emotionally, Mr. Elkins seemed to fill the position of Mr. Mathias as a best friend, as well as a teacher and guide. He sort of picked up where Mr. Mathias left off, since I haven't seen him in a couple years.

I can't describe to you in words all of how my life has changed since I met Mr. Mathias. I can only hope that what I have said can suffice. His influence upon me is undoubtedly positive. I've lived each day since then with a sense of gratitude for my love of music. However, it wasn't just the event of Kids On Broadway or just the person of Mathias; it was all the people that were there along with me during and after those years that have influenced me. I'd thank them individually, but it would take the rest of my life to name them all. Mr. Mathias is just the one name of the myriads that have had a significant impact on my life. He has his story, and I have mine. I thank him for being my teacher throughout those chapters of his life. I haven't been the same since; I'm a happier person than I could ever have been.

Persuasive Writing: *"This is what I believe and why I think you should believe it."*

The persuasive essay must first have a debatable point (open to dispute, or viewed from more than one angle). Writers usually assert and maintain a clear position throughout the piece. They present convincing evidence and explanations to clarify, expand, or support this position. They learn that any argument is only as convincing as the reasons that support it. Students may use direct or indirect quotes to give authority and support to their argument, but they must learn to distinguish hard from soft evidence. The essay should appeal to reason, acknowledge opposing views, and maintain a moderate emotional tone, and exhibit a strong voice that conveys a commitment to sharing their knowledge and point of view.

The introduction to the essay should attract and engage the readers, as well as provide a forecast. The writer should identify the issue clearly and immediately, and show the audience that this essay deserves their attention. As writers build to the thesis, they should offer significant background material so the readers are fully prepared to understand the intended position. By the end of the introduction, writers should state a clear, concrete, and *definite* thesis.

The body of the essay offers the support and refutation for the argument. Writers should arrange details, reasons, examples, and/or anecdotes in an effective, persuasive way. Effective essay writers use reasons that rest on impersonal grounds of support. They develop each supporting point with concrete, specific details (facts, examples, narratives, quotations, or other evidence that can be verified empirically or logically). In at least one separate paragraph, writers should refute opposing arguments (including any anticipated reader objection to your points).

The conclusion sums up the case and makes a direct appeal. Writers should summarize their main points and refutation, emphasizing the strongest material. They should end the essay by appealing directly to readers for a definite action (where appropriate).

To lay a foundation for persuasive writing, teachers can encourage students to present arguments orally in class as well as to write letters, editorials, and articles on controversial issues being discussed in class.

Writing Prompts that Require Persuasive Responses

The student will compose a persuasive paper attempting to persuade, convince, or inspire readers to think as the writer does.

Persuasive Prompt One

Think of a favorite place where you and your friends like to hang out. Imagine that your community is proposing to build a new shopping mall there. Write a letter to the editor of the local paper in which you establish your position for or against this proposal.

Persuasive Prompt Two

Think of one thing in your school that you would like to see changed. You might suggest changes in school rules, the cafeteria, or the building itself. Persuade your principal to act on your idea by defining the problem and explaining the reasons for the change you are proposing.

Persuasive Prompt Three

State legislators have proposed raising the driving age to 18. Write a letter expressing your views on the issue to convince your legislator to either support or oppose the change.

Persuasive Prompt Four

You have the opportunity to design a different time schedule for your high school, including such things as classes, labs, lunch, and start and stop time. Explain what your schedule would be and persuade your peers to support it in a school election by telling them how it would benefit them.

Assessing Persuasive Writing

Assess persuasive writing using a rubric that focuses on the elements of effective persuasive techniques. See *Assessment Rubric for Persuasive Writing* on page 22 and *Exemplary Student Essay for a Persuasive Prompt* on page 23.

Assessment Rubric for Persuasive Writing

Score	Meaning (focus, thesis, support)	Structure (organization, flow)	Language (correct sentences, word choice)	Audience/Style
5	The persuasive paper has a clear thesis that grows out of sufficient background and is supported with convincing evidence	The ideas are clearly organized with the ideas flowing from the thesis in a logical progression using either inductive or deductive reasoning; strong introduction, body and conclusion	The language is vivid with correct sentences and colorful word choice	At least one paragraph that refutes the opposing; strong confident voice
4	The persuasive paper has an adequate thesis, but is lacking in textual evidence and convincing support for the position	Ideas are there, but are not fully developed or do not further the thesis. Good transitions and connectors to show line of reasoning; conclusion needs creativity	The language is clear with minimal sentence and word errors	Needs to attend to reader's need for information; needs to address the opposition; writer needs to show more conviction
3	The persuasive paper has an ambiguous thesis and contains the main supporting evidence, but, there is either an unclear focus or insufficient supporting details and textual evidence	The ideas are not clear, need more elaboration and support for ideas, and/or the organization needs work. Work on better transitions; conclusion is stereotypical	There are appropriate word choices and mostly correct sentences	Needs to address reader's concerns and take a more assertive position
2	The persuasive paper has some ideas, but no clear focus and lacks details of the main events	Not enough significant ideas from the novel; lacking direction and logical progression; no appeal in the conclusion	Word choices are limited; there are errors in sentence structure	Position confusing to reader; writer shows a weak voice
1	The writing lacks clear focus and support	Jumps around; does not move from one point to another logically	Word choices are inappropriate. There are many incorrect sentences	Weak claims and no writer's voice

---

Exemplary Student Essay for Persuasive Prompt

Nathanael Litter, Student
Ruth McClain, Teacher
Paint Valley High School

Persuasive Prompt Three—Letter to Legislator

To Whom It May Concern:

I am a 17-year-old high school student who has been driving for over a year now. It has come to my attention that the state legislature is considering raising the legal driving age from 16 to 18. If that is the case, and I certainly hope that it is, I want to be the first to pledge my full support of this piece of legislation.

I believe that this change would be beneficial not only to the individual driver but to the community as well. For example, with this change in effect, it would allow younger drivers two more full years to practice their driving skills and refine their driving ability. This would, in turn, produce more experienced and mature drivers, making our highways and communities a lot safer.

With this law, I also believe that there would be a noticeable reduction in auto accidents as well as in fatalities among young people. The added experience would be invaluable, especially during hazardous driving conditions such as rain, snow, ice, and even darkness.

As a high school student, I have already been in my first wreck. It was a late December night, and I was traveling home from my girlfriend's house. As I gunned the engine to pass the car in front of me, I fishtailed and slammed into the guardrail. I didn't consider the fact that it had rained earlier that night, and the dropping temperature had caused the rain to freeze turning sections of the road into solid sheets of ice. I believe that had I received the additional two years of experience, this accident, like many others, could have been prevented.

The increased training would also allow for a greater understanding and knowledge of our traffic laws and the mechanics of the road. I know that I don't always take precautions when driving, and sometimes, when I'm in a hurry, I don't even notice the speed limit or the various other warning signs on the road. Being 17, I realize that the new law would have affected me, *and I would not be allowed to drive yet. However, the experience gained would be invaluable in creating safe and responsible drivers, and that's what I want to be.*

I do hope that you will consider these thoughts very seriously.

Sincerely,
Nathanael Litter
Paint Valley High School

Literary or Aesthetic Writing:
"This is how I have shaped my ideas about what I have seen, experienced, or imagined."

According to Claggett (1996), any writing growing out of the previous purposes may move into the aesthetic realm when the work is crafted into an art form such as story, poem, or essay. In this type of writing, the purpose can also be reflecting, informing, or persuading. Even though many teachers ask students to write stories, quite often the instruction is lacking and students do little more than retell movies or stories that they had heard.

Narrative pieces engage readers with a story line and enable them to enter the writer's real or imaginary world. Narrative writing is characterized by scenes that move through time. It requires writers to establish a situation or setting; develop believable characters, either real or imagined; and tell what happened. Storywriters use narrative strategies such as dialogue, description, sensory detail, and concrete language to create an event or experience for the reader. Narration is the primary mode for developing autobiographical incidents as well as fiction. It is an important strategy used in other types of writing such as biographical, informative, and persuasive writing. For more ideas, see *Portfolio Assessment: Short Story Portfolio* for Ruggieri's preparation and development of story writing and character development.

Assessing Aesthetic or Literary Writing

According to Claggett (1996, p. 70), it is impossible to design a rubric that extends to all forms of aesthetic or literary writing because nearly all kinds of writing may be elevated to that level. There are rubrics for specific genres located throughout the rest of this volume for poetry, research, art, short story, etc. The following assessment elicits narrative writing resulting from responding to a prompt.

Writing Prompts that Require Narrative Responses

The student will compose a narrative that describes an actual event or tells an imaginary story, depending on the selected prompt.

Narrative Prompt One

Compose a personal narrative that recreates a first-time experience. Be certain to include one or more characters, dialogue, a setting, and other devices such as foreshadowing, suspense, and similes.

Narrative Prompt Two

Imagine you could meet someone you admire. Write a narrative in which you describe what you would do in a day to help this person get to know you.

Narrative Prompt Three

Narrate the events of a day in your life from the perspective of an article of your clothing.

Narrative Prompt Four

Imagine that you have a photograph in your hand. Tell the story of the photograph.

Assessing Aesthetic Writing: Narrative

The effective narrative writer engages the reader by establishing a story situation and by assuming a narrative stance or point of view. The writer develops the story through characterization and narrative strategies such as flashbacks, foreshadowing, and withholding information to establish suspense. See *Assessment Rubric for Narrative Response to a Prompt* on page 26 and *Exemplary Student Essay for a Narrative Prompt* on page 27.

Assessment Rubric for Narrative Response to a Prompt

	4	*3*	*2*	*1*
Introduction	Establishes the setting; sets the tone; introduces main character; establishes area of conflict; foreshadows the ending	Establishes the setting; introduces the main characters; the conflict or stressful is not obvious; does not foreshadow the ending	Describes the setting and the main character; the stressful situation is missing; there is no foreshadowing	Description is too brief to visualize the setting and/or the main character. No allusion to the stress or conflict
Body	Tells story in scenes. Develops characters through action and dialogue; shows us what is going on; develops plot through increasingly serious problems; makes solutions of problems appropriate to the characters	Tells the story in a series of scenes that contain a purpose, an obstacle or conflict, and a resolution; characters are developed mostly through action rather than dialogue; solutions are appropriate to the characters	Tells story in exposition; interesting plot and characters, though not as fully developed as could be; some use of effective dialogue to carry the action; solution of problems is realistic; some repetition of details	Tells us, rather than shows us, the plot and characters; limited plot and character development; no use of dialogue; solutions not appropriate to the characters; repetition of details; telegraphed the punches
Conclusion	Presents a final, crucial conflict, a creative climax that reveals something to readers that was not obvious or predictable	Presents an interesting, unexpected climax; surprise ending	Conclusion is somewhat predictable, but is appropriate for the story	Conclusion is too obvious, predictable, and unimaginative
Dialogue	Speech advances the story, revealing something new about the plot or the character; punctuated correctly; speech evokes the characters' personalities and motivations; characters speak naturally	Speech advances the story plot and the characters; punctuation is correct; speeches are concise; speech is used to convey character and develop conflict	Speech conveys the character, but the writer bogs down in chatter that does not advance the story; some errors in punctuation	Too many "he said," "she said," phrases; incorrect indentation and punctuation; speech does not reveal something new about the plot or character; too much direct address
Narrative Strategies	Uses effective strategies such as foreshadowing, suspense, analogy, flashback	Shows some use of narrative strategies; shows control of the movement of the story	Limited understanding of narrative strategies; lacks control of the story's movement	No understanding of narrative strategy; random undeveloped ideas

Language/ Style	Uses image, metaphor, and simile effectively; uses sentence variety; uses active voice; consistent style, tone, and point of view; grammatically correct; fluent prose; strong narrative voice; uses symbolism	Rich use of language to convey the story; uses active voice and sentence variety; mostly correct use of grammar; strong narrative voice	Limited use of language skills to convey the story; uses some passive voice; makes some errors in spelling and mechanics; narrative voice is emerging	Uses trite phrases, clichés, passive voice; limited use of language; incorrect sentences and misspellings; lack of sentence variety; voice is hidden or silenced
Prompt Connections	The paper is clearly focused on the prompt	The paper is generally related to the prompt	The paper is somewhat related to the prompt	The paper is only slightly connected to the prompt

Exemplary Student Essay for Narrative Prompt

Laura Garofali, Student
Nicole McBurney, Teacher
Brookfield High School

Narrative Prompt One—First Time Experience

I will never forget the first time I went driving. It was a sticky, hot July day when my mother finally gave into my demand about me getting my permit to drive. I felt nervous and excited all at once; nervous because I have never driven before, and excited because now the idea was dawning on my parents that I wasn't their little girl anymore, and therefore, I am entitled to some freedom and responsibility.

My mother drove me to the Driver's License Bureau where I had to take a test before I could receive my permit to drive. I spent an hour waiting in a small, white room that looked like one of the rooms where people with mental problems and straight jackets spent their time. Then, I forgot to pick a number. So I went over to the red number dispenser and picked the number 102. A half an hour later, the old lady, that reminded me of a dried up prune all covered with wrinkles, at the front desk screeched my number. I came up to the desk and the old lady with the scratchy voice gave me the test and told me to take a seat over by the wooden desk in the far, left hand corner of the room. The wooden chair seemed to stab me as I sat down. When I was done, I went back up to the desk where the old lady sat and handed her the test. Nervously I watched as she pulled out a red marker and started to go through the answers, marking one then another. When she was done she handed me a pink and yellow paper that said that I had passed my permit test.

Happy to have that done and over with, I ran out of the Driver's License Bureau to our red, Plymouth minivan and demanded to drive home, but being the over protective person that she is, my mother said that I had to practice a little first. We drove to the school and drove in circles in the school parking lot for what seemed like a hundred times. Finally, she said that I was allowed to drive home. Palms sweating, I took control of the wheel, and the bright sun blinded my eyes.

"Put your seat belt on and check your mirrors" demanded my mother.

"Ma, I know what to do, just calm down and let me get the car started." I said with a sigh as I turned the car key and stepped on the gas.

"Slow down! We're in the school parking lot; it's only 5mph." she complained.

"No one goes 5mph, and besides, the parking lot is empty."

I came out of the parking lot and made a left turn to go to the intersection. Not used to stopping, I came to the red light, and instead of coming to a nice, gradual stop, I slammed on the brakes and came to a sudden stop. Talk about whiplash! I started to laugh at my mother because she didn't wear her seat belt, and her head just missed the dashboard. She turned to me and gave me one of those looks; the look that said, "If you ever want to get out of your room and see the light of day again, then shut your mouth." I quickly shut my mouth and focused on driving. The light turned green, and I stepped on the gas.

"You better get rid of that led foot young lady," replied my mother.

"Ma, the speed limit is 60, and I'm going 55mph."

"You have only been driving for forty-five minutes; you don't have to go the speed limit right away."

Up ahead I was supposed to turn off the highway, so I put on my turning signal. I was getting closer, and closer to the turn, and I can tell my mother was getting more and more aggravated from my speed.

"Slow down, you're turning soon!"

To avoid an argument and getting grounded, I slowed down a little.

"Slow down more." she complained.

"Calm down, I know what I am doing."

"Don't look at me, look at the road," she said, always getting the last word in as usual. Angry, I turned right sharp, going about 40mph. The car jolted to the right.

"Holy crap!" I yelled. I could have sworn we were going to tip right over, but to my surprise, the van stayed on all four wheels.

"Slow down and focus on the road or else you won't be driving for a long time!" she warned angrily.

After about ten minutes, the tension passed and we started a boring conversation about school. Then, up ahead, I saw a fuzzy, little, brown thing that ran onto the road. It looked like a big, hairball.

"What the... hey, mom, there's a squirrel or something on the road up ahead."

"When we get closer just honk your horn and slow down a little," she answered back.

As we got closer, it was confirmed that it was a squirrel. Struck with terror, the squirrel didn't move, so I slowed down and honked the horn.

"Ah, mom, it's not moving. This squirrel better not want to play chicken with a car."

"Oh, it'll move." she said calmly as we approached it twenty feet away; then ten feet, then five feet. I slowed down more and I closed my eyes half of a second, and "bump," we hit it.

"Oh, no. I killed the poor, little, woodland, creature! You said it would move, but it didn't! Stupid squirrel, I better not have to wash the car when we get home." I complained.

"Don't worry, I'll have your brother wash it" she said. I laughed at the image of my brother standing there with the hose wondering what the stuff on the front of the car was.

That was the first time I went driving and killed something all in one day, but as the saying goes, "Hey, if it's on the road, it's free territory." Meanwhile, I still never got over that lead foot problem, and my driving makes all the passengers sick, and if someone one pukes in my car, he cleans it up, or else.... But on the plus side, I never hit another squirrel again, well, not yet anyway.

Bibliography

Beach, R. (1993). *A teacher's introduction to reader-response theories.* Urbana, IL: NCTE.

Britton, J., Burgess, T., Martin, N., McLeod, A., & Rosen, H. (1977). *The development of writing abilities (11—18).* Hong Kong: Macmillan Education.

Claggett, F. *A measure of success: From assignment to assessment in English language arts.* Portsmouth, NH: Heinemann Boynton/Cook Publishers.

Moffett, J. (1981). *Active voice: A writing program across the curriculum.* Upper Montclair, NJ: Boynton/Cook Publishers.

Ohio Department of Education. (2001). *High school proficiency testing: Fact sheets.*

Rosenblatt, L. (1995). *Literature as exploration.* New York: Modern Language Association.

Part II

Portfolio (Collections) Assessment

3

CHARACTER BROCHURE

Janie Reinart

By helping to focus the student's attention upon the actual emotions through which he has entered into the lives of others, the teacher can reinforce the power of literature to develop social imagination.

Louise Rosenblatt

Overview of Authentic Learning

How do students make meaning of literature, and, by writing, become an integral part of the text? Using reader response, students clarify feelings and thoughts about personal convictions while looking at, and taking on, the identities of the characters in the story. This project involves creating a brochure featuring a character from a book. Ideas for the text are taken from daily journal writing and observations from the short story or book they have chosen to read. Students cut and paste pictures and handwrite text to lay out a rough draft for the brochure. Then students use technology to create the final draft of a two-sided, tri-fold brochure with pictures. When completed, students present the brochure to the class. The rating scale included with this assessment is teacher-created, but students might benefit by creating criteria of their own for the project. Upon completion, students will display brochures for all to enjoy. Modeling is important! Teachers are encouraged to create a brochure to share with the class.

NCTE/IRA Standards

During this unit, STUDENTS WILL:

♦ Select and read a short story or novel. In doing so, students will read a wide range of print and nonprint texts to build an understanding of texts, of themselves, and of the cultures of the U.S. and the world (NCTE/IRA Standard #1).

♦ Create a character brochure. As such, students will apply a wide range of strategies to comprehend, interpret, evaluate, and appreciate texts (NCTE/IRA Standard #3); they will use a variety of technological and informational resources to gather and synthesize information and to create and communicate knowledge (NCTE/IRA Standard #8); and students will use spoken, written, and visual language to accomplish their own purposes (NCTE/IRA Standards #12).

♦ In daily journals employ a wide range of strategies as they write using different writing process elements appropriately to communicate for a variety of purposes (NCTE/IRA Standard #5) and they will apply knowledge of language structure, language conventions, media techniques, figurative language, and genre to create, critique, and discuss print and nonprint texts (NCTE/IRA Standard #6).

Materials

♦ Examples of brochures
♦ Writing prompts
♦ Journals
♦ Story
♦ Digital camera
♦ Regular camera
♦ Directions and rubric
♦ Template
♦ Character map
♦ Computer lab

Performance Tasks

Read a Book and Select a Character

Teacher selects a variety of short stories or novels for students to read. Selections might be read as a whole class or in Daniels' Literature Circles (1994). (Visit Jim Burke's Web site and download a packet that includes an overview and role sheets for this activity: http://www.englishcompanion.com/pdf Docs/ litcirclepacket.pdf. As students read the story, and keep a daily journal, they will eventually select one character. Ask students to make a Character Card Bookmark for the character they selected. For information about this, visit Jim Burke's Web site and download the template: http://www.englishcompanion.com/pdfDocs/toolcharcardbmark.pdf.

When the reading is complete, ask students to create a character map for the character they selected. See Figure 3.1 Character Map Assignment, page 39.

Directions and Assessment

The teacher hands out the directions and the rating scale with the due date of the project. Project time is flexible and can vary between four to six weeks or longer, as needed. See *Brochure Assignment Sheet* on page 37 and *Assessment Rubric for Character Brochure* on page 38.

Brochure Specifications

Each brochure will include or be created as follows:
- ◆ Five pictures and/or drawings.
- ◆ The front page displays a photograph of the character. Book character pictures can be cut from magazines or drawn. Students can also pose in costume to create character pictures.
- ◆ Students will write about nine different topics.
- ◆ Student names are on each brochure.

Suggestions

Use a digital camera to scan in pictures. The themes for additional photos can include a character snapshot, a family portrait, a picture of the character's friends, or an activity the book character would enjoy. Schedule time in computer lab for creating brochures.

Analyze Commercial Brochures

Students need to bring in sample brochures that feature a product, support a candidate, advertise a business, or explore a vacation. In small groups, students analyze sample brochures to identify elements that make the material attractive, interesting, and informative. Small groups report findings to the large group. The class discusses elements of design, layout, and color. Students create a mock page layout of their brochure (see Figures 3.2 (p. 40) and 3.3 (p. 41) page-layout templates).

Daily Journals

Students write in their journals during class or for homework using a journal page that is folded in half lengthwise. Based upon the topic for the day, one-half of the page contains the student's perspective while the other half represents the mind and hearts of different book characters. Each writing prompt is a potential section for choosing a character for the brochure.

Journal Writing Prompts

The teacher gives daily journal writing prompts, as the story is being read and discussed in class.

Prompts might include:

- Essential information, from eye color to special events, such as birthdays or school activities
- Who the character is and what she/he likes or dislikes
- Mannerisms, gestures, language, voice of the character
- Favorites or pet peeves
- What the character is proud of or ashamed of
- What the character believes in
- What she/he does in free time
- Dominant personality trait
- Mentors for the character
- What the character would like to learn or achieve
- The character's future
- Students create their own categories

Editing

Students:

- Revise content and grammar
- Edit spelling, and punctuation
- Have three classmates proof work
- Print and hand in their final draft

Presentation

Students:

- Prepare to present their brochure to share with the class
- Practice presentation with a partner
- Present to class

Bibliography

Corcoran, B. (Ed.). (1994). *Knowledge in the making.* Portsmouth, NH: Heinemann.

Daniels, H. (1994). *Literature circles: Voice and choice in the student-centered classroom.* York, ME: Stenhouse Publishers.

Making a personal brochure. (1992). Fort Collins, CO: Cottonwood Press.

Assignment Sheet for Making a Character Brochure

Making a Character Brochure

This brochure is going to be about one of the main characters in the short story or novel that we are reading:_____

_____. The brochure will include five pictures or drawings. On the front page, you will put a photo of your character (this can be cut out from a magazine or scanned in with use of a digital camera, or a portrait done in colored pencils). The other photographs can include a childhood picture, a family portrait, and a picture of the character with some friends from work or a picture of the character and /or friends taking part in an activity they enjoy. You may substitute a drawing of a symbol that best represents your character for one of the photos.

The brochure must include at least nine paragraphs (each a different topic) taken from your daily journal writing. Fill out character map and journal entries as if you were that person or character. Expand and revise your work. Title each paragraph. Start with a paragraph that gives a brief description of the character. End with a paragraph that shows the character's future and goals. Pick seven other paragraphs. Use the template of the brochure to make a rough draft. The brochure needs to be typed. Use your skills to make the brochure uniquely your character's own reflection of his/her life. Have three classmates edit your brochure before you turn in the corrected final copy.

Assessment Rubric for Character Brochure

	Beginner 1 point	Novice 2 points	Intermediate 3 points	Expert 4 points	Self-Evaluation
Content of the Characterization	Includes little essential information and only one or two facts about the character	Includes some essential information with few citations and few facts about the character	Includes essential information with most sources properly cited. Includes enough elaboration to give readers an understanding of the character	Covers character completely and in depth. Includes properly cited sources and complete information. Encourages readers to know more	
Technical Requirements	Includes less than five paragraphs and fewer than three pictures or drawings; might still be in the rough draft stage	Includes less than nine paragraphs and fewer than four pictures or drawings that are electronically generated	Includes nine well-written paragraphs and at least four pictures or drawings that are electronically generated	Includes nine informative paragraphs and five creative graphics that are electronically generated	
Mechanics	Includes more than 5 grammatical errors, misspellings, or punctuation errors	Includes 3 to 4 grammatical errors, misspellings, or punctuation errors	Includes 2 to 3 grammatical errors, misspellings, or punctuation errors	Grammar, spelling, punctuation, capitalization are correct. No errors in the text	
Visual Presentation	Little visual appeal resulting from lack of color, messy layout and poor organization. Not neat	Brochure lacks visual appeal that results from inappropriate use of color; unbalanced layout and lack of organization	Brochure is visually appealing, well-organized, and neat. Layout is appropriate	Brochure is colorful, neat, interesting, creative and unique. Layout is effective and balanced	
Oral Presentation	Great difficulty communicating ideas. Poor voice projection. Little preparation or incomplete work	Some difficulty communicating ideas, due to voice projection, lack of preparation, or incomplete work	Communicates ideas with proper voice projection. Adequate preparation and delivery	Communicates ideas with enthusiasm, proper voice projection, appropriate language, and clear delivery	

TOTAL POINTS

Scale: 18–20 = Expert; 15–17 = Intermediate; 10–14 = Novice; 6–9 = Beginner

Figure 3.1 Character Map

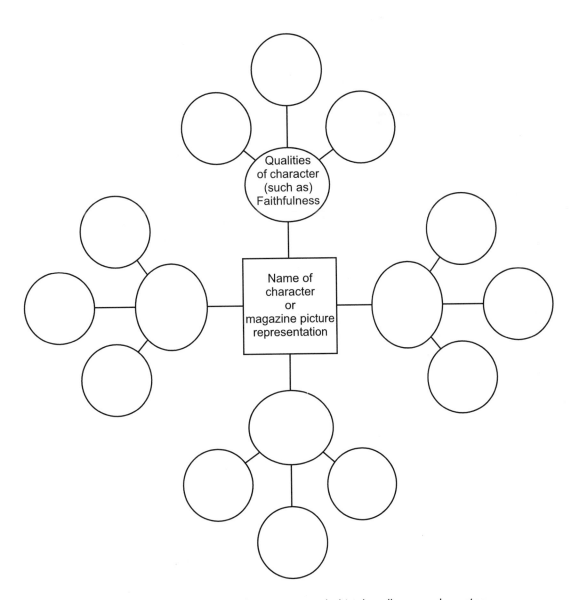

Note: Add as many more clusters as needed to describe your character.

Figure 3.2 Template for First Side of Brochure

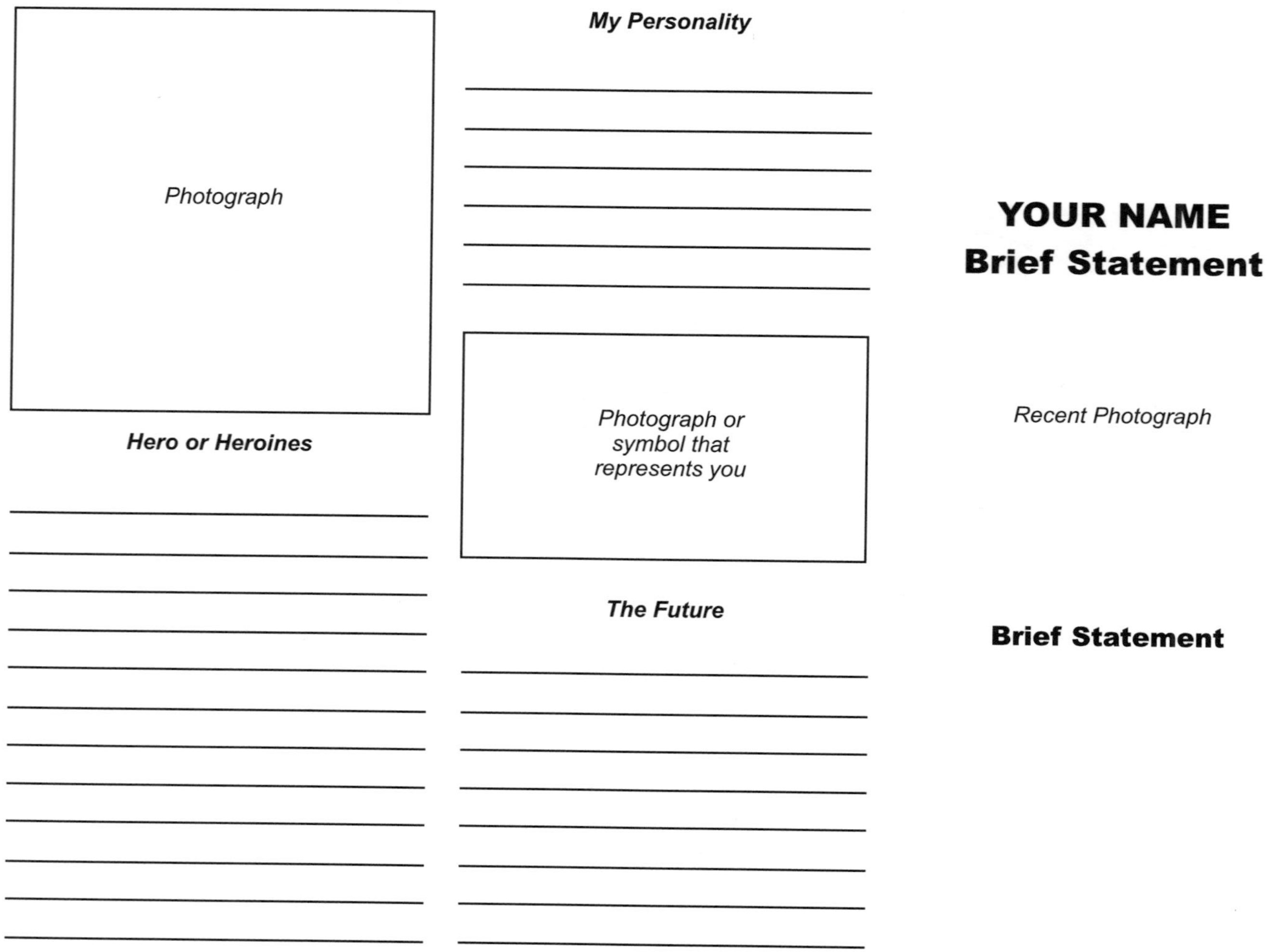

YOUR NAME
Brief Statement

Recent Photograph

Brief Statement

My Personality

Photograph or symbol that represents you

The Future

Photograph

Hero or Heroines

Figure 3.3 Template for Second Side of Brochure

ME: In a nutshell

When I Was A Baby

Photograph

My Early Childhood

My Favorites

Little Known Facts

Pet Peeves

Photograph

4

CHARACTER PORTFOLIO

Jacqueline Glasgow

*Curiosity is one of the permanent and
certain characteristics of a vigorous mind.*

Samuel Johnson

Overview of Authentic Learning

In a student-centered classroom, students take responsibility for their learning, for constructing meaning from their experiences. According to Daniels and Bizar, "Expression, in all of its manifold forms, is a key to learning and thinking" (1998, p.9). The character portfolio provides students with the opportunity to express their understanding of either a main character from a novel or a fictional character that they might later use to write a short story.

NCTE/IRA Standards

In creating this portfolio, students will use the expressive arts to create a collage, a resume, a character map and/or a coat of arms for the character they wish to portray. This project requires students to apply a wide range of strategies to comprehend, interpret, evaluate, and appreciate texts (NCTE/IRA Standard #3). This portfolio also requires students to adjust their use of spoken, written, and visual language (e.g., conventions, style, vocabulary) to communicate effectively with a variety of audiences and for different purposes (NCTE/IRA Standard #4).

Planned Performance Tasks

The student examples for these activities were taken from Lyn Bruner's portfolio for Magnolia April Pugh in Spite Fences by Trudy Krisher (1999). Spite Fences is a coming-of-age story set against the rural South during the early Civil Rights movement. Thirteen-year-old Maggie Pugh has lived in Kinship, Georgia, all her life, but after the summer of 1960, it doesn't seem like the same place. It's the summer of Maggie witnessing a terrible act against a black man she had come to think of as a special friend. Most of all it's the summer of Maggie's first camera, a tool that becomes a way for her to find independence and a different kind of truth.

Creating/Visualizing Characters through Resumes

A good way to begin developing characters is to brainstorm ideas and develop a character resume. Consider the following categories, as well as ideas that you would add to the list. Through the resume, you can help a reader visualize what your character looks like, understand how your character behaves, and appreciate what motivates your character to particular actions. Once you have brainstormed the basics, you will have a foundation for further developing your characters. See *Character Resume Template* on page 45, adapted from Crawford Kilian's Advice on Novel Writing, and Lyn Bruner's *Resume for Magnolia Pugh in Krisher's Spite Fences*, on page 46.

Coat of Arms (Writing Frame and Poster)

Choose a main/fictional character from the story to feature on a coat of arms. Complete the writing frame for generating the symbols for the coat of arms. Then construct the coat of arms using symbols created from the metaphors. See *Writing Frame of Coat of Arms*, and Lyn Bruner's *Writing Frame for Maggie Pugh in Krisher's Spite Fences* on page 47.

Writing Frame Template for Coat of Arms

If _____were an object, it would be _____, because _____

If _____were a word, it would be _____, because _____

If _____were an emotion, it would be _____, because _____

If _____were a day of the week, it would be _____, because _____

If _____were a color, it would be _____, because _____

If _____were a song, it would be _____, because _____

If _____were an animal, it would be _____, because _____

If _____were a plant, it would be _____, because _____

If _____were a season, it would be _____, because _____

If _____were a time of day, it would be _____, because _____

Character Resume Template

Name/Address/Phone Number:

Date/Place of Birth:

Physical Description (height/weight/hair/eyes):

Family (married/single, children, relatives):

Hobbies/Interests:

Pets:

Education: Employment:

Wages/Salary:

Ethnicity:

Religion:

Dreams for the Future:

Problems/Hardships:

Friends:

Musical Taste:

Preferred Clothing Style:

Personality (shy/outgoing, etc.):

Favorite Foods:

Enemies:

Positive Personal Habits (organized, sloppy, etc.):

Undesirable Personal Habits (procrastinator, etc.):

Vacations:

Home (apartment/house/alone/with others):

Rural/City Lifestyle:

Conservative/Liberal Beliefs:

Motivated/Apathetic:

Calm/Quick-tempered:

Fears:

Attitude toward Life:

Attitude toward Death:

Materialistic/Appreciative of Simple Things:

Nature Lover/Unappreciative of Simple Things:

Observant/Oblivious:

Carefree/Guarded:

Sense of Humor/No Sense of Humor:

Philosophy of Life (in a phrase):

Resume for Magnolia Pugh

Character Resume
Magnolia April Pugh

Address:	EXMOOR 6281	
Date & Place of Birth:	April, 1947 Kinship, Georgia	
Physical Description:	Tall and strong. Long, thick, auburn hair. Rounded eyebrows over deep brown eyes and a wide upper lip that jutted out over the lower lip like a cliff.	
Citizenship/ Ethnic Origin:	US Citizen	
Parents' Names and Occupations:	Henry Pugh	Former salesman for Johnson & Johnson, future handyman
	Izabelle Pugh	Housewife
	One sister:	Gardenia June Pugh
Friends Names and Occupations:	Pert Wilson:	Waitress
	Ezekiel Jeremiah Freeman (Zeke):	Town peddler
	George Andrew Hardy, Ph.D.	Assistant Professor of Mathematics
Social Class:	Lower class	
Salary:	$10.00/week	Worked two days a week for George Hardy cleaning and delivering important messages and packages.
Job-Related Skills:	Trustworthiness, dependability, and loyalty	
Hobbies/ Recreation:	Photography and going on "sneaks" with her best friend, Pert Wilson	
Ambitions:	To be a professional photographer	
Fears and Anxieties:	Virgil Boggs, her mother, and that she might never be able to see the truth clearly.	
Most Painful Setback/Disappointment:	The view from the tree of Zeke's abuse at the hands of Virgil Boggs. "I felt the salt rising behind my eyes at my secret, my own terrible secret. And I stopped praying from that night on." (p.188)	
Attitude Toward Life:	Pessimistic	
Attitude Toward Death:	Not fearful of death, to her it might have been a relief .	
Philosophy of Life (in a phrase):	"To prejudge other men's notions before we have looked into them is not to show their darkness but to put out our own eyes."	

Writing Frame for Coat of Arms Maggie Pugh

Writing Frame for Coat of Arms for Maggie Pugh
in Krisher's Spite Fences

If Maggie were:

an object, it would be an ax to chop down fences.

a word, it would be cautious until she could become strong enough to walk in the truths she learned.

an emotion, it would be fear because she was not certain she would ever have the courage to speak the truth.

a day of the week, it would be Sunday, because it is the beginning of the week.

a color, it would be red for the rage she felt toward Virgil Boggs for his vindictive and cruel actions.

a song, it would be "Honesty" by Billy Joel because she, too, experienced that "if you look for truthfulness, you might just as well be blind. It always seemed to be so hard to find."

an animal, it would be a turtle. Her fears and the injustices she experienced caused her to live in a shell.

a plant, it would be a Magnolia tree which starts out very weak and fragile and then grows strong and unwavering.

a season, it would be spring because spring represents new life and new beginnings.

a time of day, it would be dawn, because "after the darkness," then comes the dawn.

Now create the coat of arms to represent the images you have created in your imagination. See Lyn Bruner's Coat of Arms for Maggie in Krisher's Spite Fences on page 48.

Collage and Explanation

An alternative assignment for the coat of arms is to create a collage. Considering the images you have generated about the motivation, behavior, and physical characteristics for your character, create an artistic collage from magazines or clipart that portrays your character's personality, interests, appearance, etc.

Coat of Arms for Maggie

Character Map and Explanation

In this assignment you will probe characters and the story context by mapping them according to their relationships. You are not making comparisons so much as uncovering strong relationships between characters and how those are webbed together to create a whole story. Make separate symbols to represent each character in the book. Begin by connecting the most obvious pairs or trios, ones who obviously belong together because: they relate to the central character in a similar way, by their close personal relationship, or by their antipathy for one another. Label the ways that characterize the relationships for pairs, trios, etc. You may show the emotional relationships by color-coding the lines that go from one character to another. Create a key to represent the colors and/or symbols. Write an explanation describing your choices. See Lyn Bruner's *Character Map for Krisher's Spite Fences*.

Character Map for *Spite Fences*

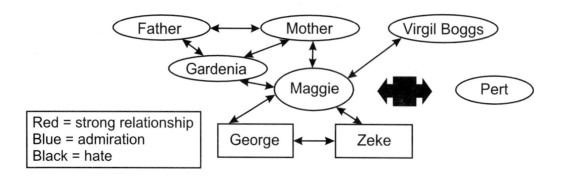

Assessment Rubric for Art Projects

	Distinguished 4 Points	Proficient 3 Points	Adequate 2 Points	Beginner 1 Point	Score
Ingenuity and Idea	Inventive: fully developed ideas. Uses unique symbol system. Has five or more symbols in it.	Excellent ideas. Uses some original symbols. Has at least 4 symbols.	Symbols are somewhat original. Has at least 3 symbols.	Unoriginal. Did not go beyond common notions and symbols. Uses two or less symbols.	__ x4__ (16)
Craftmanship	Shows mastery of media chosen; careful attention to detail quality of the representation.	Strong use of the media chosen. Some attention paid to detail.	Shows effort at learning new techniques. Could use more attention to details. Could use more finishing touches.	Lacks effort in learning new techniques. Needs improvement. Lacks pride and effort in finished work.	__ x6__ (24)
Use of Principles and Elements of Design	Innovative use of texture and color. Size and layering is purposeful and adds to the overall quality of the piece.	Uses required principles and elements. Not all uses are justified.	Uses most of the required principles and elements. Lacks some purpose in design.	Poor planning of principles and elements of design. Does not include all required principles and elements.	__ x 7__ (28)
Concepts and Content	Artwork excels in communicating ideas to the viewer. Uses assignment requirements.	Artwork reflects development of ideas and thoughts, and communicates well with the viewer.	Artwork reflects ideas but does not fully communicate these ideas to the viewer.	Artwork lacks ideas, does not communicate with the viewer.	__ x8__ (32)

Scale: 90-100 = A; 80-89 = B; 70-79 = C; 60-69 = D   Total Score: Final Grade:

Performance Assessment

To assess a project that is comprised of expressive arts, the following criteria is utilized: the ideas and ingenuity used to convey the message, the quality of craftsmanship, the principles and elements of design (color, shape, form, line, shading, texture) and the complexity of the content. See *Assessment Rubric for Art Projects* on page 49.

Bibliography

Daniels, H., & Bizar, M. (1998). *Methods that matter: Six structures for best practice classrooms.* York, ME: Stenhouse Publishers.

Kilian, C. (April 2001). *Advice on Novel Writing* [Online]. Available: http://www.steampunk.com/sfch/writing/ckilian/

Krisher, T. (1999). *Spite Fences.* New York: Econo-Clad Books.

Olson, C., & Schiesl, S. A multiple intelligences approach to teaching multicultural literature. *Language Arts Journal of Michigan,* 1, 12, 21–28.

5

CYBER JOURNALING FOR JUSTICE

Jacqueline Glasgow

Only Robinson Crusoe had everything done by Friday.

Anonymous

Overview of Authentic Learning

How do we imagine schooling for a democratic society? I imagine a schooling that embraces the critical literacy perspective: it begins with the problems and needs of the students, it challenges them with multiple realities of life, and it encourages them to take action against injustice. To become aware of inequities, I have structured my Young Adult Literature course based on books that reflect issues on equity and social justice. I pair my students with high school students who choose the books for their cyber journal project. Students use e-mail, digital cameras, and CUSEEME Videoconferencing to discuss the book, research the issues raised, and complete a Microsoft PowerPoint presentation. Then, as a social action assignment, students create one of their PowerPoint slides as a public awareness announcement to inform people about the injustice presented in their book. At the end of the project, students from both schools get together for a pizza party and collaborate in making a character continuum.

Standards

During this unit, students will:

♦ Select a young adult novel to read and to discuss with a student from a different school. In doing so, students will apply a wide range of strategies to comprehend, interpret, evaluate, and appreciate texts (NCTE/IRA Standard #3); they will adjust their use of spoken, written, and visual language to communicate effectively with a variety of audiences and for different purposes (NCTE/IRA Standard #4); and, they will employ a wide range of strategies as they write and use different writing process elements appropriately to communicate with different audiences for a variety of purposes (NCTE/IRA Standard #5).

♦ Create a Microsoft PowerPoint presentation on their reading and research of a social issue to share with their buddy and the class. In doing so, students will apply knowledge of language structure, language conventions, media techniques, figurative language, and genre to create, critique, and discuss print and nonprint texts (NCTE/IRA Standard #6); they will conduct research on issues and interest by generating ideas and questions, and by posing problems (NCTE/IRA Standard #7); they will use a variety of technological and information resources to gather and synthesize information and to create and communicate knowledge (NCTE/IRA Standard #8); they will develop an understanding of and respect for diversity in language use, patterns, and dialects across cultures, ethnic groups, geographic regions, and social roles (NCTE/IRA Standard #9); they will participate as knowledgeable, reflective, creative, and critical members of a variety of literacy communities (NCTE/IRA Standard # 11); and, they will use spoken, written, and visual language to accomplish their own purposes (NCTE/IRA Standard #12).

Planned Performance Tasks

Select a teacher from a high school with a class that is approximately the same size as yours for this project. You will need to agree on the booklist. I recommend asking the younger students to select the book first, and then match them up with the older students. Every student must have an e-mail account and scheduled time in a computer lab equipped with Microsoft PowerPoint or HyperStudio.

♦ Students choose a cyber buddy from a different high school who agrees to read the same young adult novel from the list as you. In an e-mail message, introduce yourself to your new friend.

♦ *Books must be read by _____.*

♦ Establish a reading schedule suitable to both partners in which students correspond back and forth at least twice a week (8 to 10 entries).

♦ Ask students to date and sign each entry and record inclusive page numbers. They need to print out both their own e-mail and their cyber buddy's e-mail for their portfolio.

♦ As students read the book, ask them to write comments, ask questions, and discuss insights that occur to them in their e-mail correspondence.

♦ The cyber buddy then responds to the e-mail, making comments or asking questions of her/his own.

♦ Advise students to be sensitive and responsive to their cyber buddy's e-mail entries.

♦ Students should continue reading and responding back and forth, chapter by chapter, as many times as time allows.

♦ Then, ask students to research the social justice issue presented in their book and create a Microsoft PowerPoint presentation that reflects their reading and research on the topic.

♦ Ask students to critique their cyber buddy's PowerPoint presentation.

♦ Then, ask students to write a reflective paper discussing their reactions and insights to the shared experiences.

♦ At the end, students submit their cyber journal e-mail, projects and diskette in a portfolio.

♦ If there is to be a joint get together, ask students to prepare the Report Sack assignment for the ice-breaker at the meeting or pizza party.

Microsoft PowerPoint Slide Show

Ask students to create a Microsoft PowerPoint presentation based on the theme, social problem research, characterization, poetic responses, timeline, book review, or other information they wish to include. Students should learn to use automatic timing, animation, sounds, and musical backgrounds to enhance the quality of their presentation. These shows can be burned to a CD-Rom or uploaded on a Web site for all to view and appreciate. Students should capture the highlights of their e-mails in the slides they construct. The following are assignments for slides based on Gardner's Multiple Intelligences. More detailed information about these assignments may be found at http://dragonbbs.com/members/1836.

Character Continuum and Explanation

Reflect on the relationship of characters (one to another) by locating them on different continua. The continua may be from bold to cautious; from good to evil; from just to tyrannical; or any other extremes represented in the book. Place characters' names on a line that represents movement from one extreme of the idea to the other. Then create a slide describing your placement of the characters on the continuum and how the dynamic character might change positions as the result of the events in the story.

Collage and Explanation

Ask students to create a collage of graphics or magazine images to portray the social justice issues of their book. This collage can be a slide in their PowerPoint presentation or a poster. If students make posters, take a picture of the posters with the digital camera to attach to an e-mail to share with their cyber buddies. Students should write an explanation for the images they chose.

Illustrated Poem (I Am, Bio, Found) and Explanation

For templates for these poems (I Am, Bio, and Found), see http://dragonbbs.com/members/1836.

Ask students to write an original poem using one of these templates or a form they create. Students should illustrate the poem using graphics that help carry the meaning or provide an interpretation for the poem. See Lyn Bruner's *Bio-Poem* on page 55 from her PowerPoint Presentation on Krisher's Spite Fences. Spite Fences (1999) is a coming-of-age story for thirteen-year-old Maggie Pugh during the Civil Rights movement. She befriends Zeke, an activist black trader, who draws her into the conflict of a lunch-counter strike. With camera in hand, she exposes the atrocities of the racial inequities.

Illustrated Quote from the Text and Explanation

Ask students to select a quote from the novel that is especially meaningful to them in regard to the social justice issue being addressed. Then, ask them to illustrate the quote graphically. Students need to write an explanation of their choice of quote and the representation. See Lyn Bruner's *PowerPoint Illustrated Quote for Krisher's Spite Fences* on page 55.

Original Metaphor and Explanation

There are many metaphors and symbols in a story that describe the main character. Ask students to think of a metaphor for the main character. They need to create a visual representation for the metaphor and then write a brief explanation of the image they chose. See Lyn Bruner's *PowerPoint Original Metaphor for Krisher's Spite Fences* on page 55.

Bio Poem: Ezekiel Jeremiah

Bio Poem
(From Spite Fences by Trudy Krisher)

Ezekiel Jeremiah

Proud, brave, strong and gentle

Lover of truth, justice and equality

Who feels pain, sorrow and grief
Who needs his voice to be heard, his people to be free,

and justice to be served

Who fears ignorance, Sheriff Keiter's night stick, and

that fences will be permanent fixtures in his town.

Who gives hope, strength and encouragement to his

beloved friend Maggie

Who would like to see an end to racial hatred and

discrimination and a new life for Maggie,

Resident of Kinship, Georgia

Freeman

Illustrated Quote for Krisher's *Spite Fences*
Original Metaphor for Krisher's *Spite Fences*

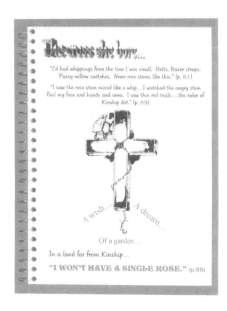

Public Awareness Announcement

After researching their social justice issue, ask students to create a slogan and graphic to inform the public of this issue, i.e., safety issues, hotlines, support groups, etc. If appropriate, encourage them to use direct quotes from the book, to raise public consciousness concerning the social justice issue. Students should use a combination of text, graphics, or perhaps animation to present their message. See Lyn Bruner's *PowerPoint presentation of Public Awareness Announcement for Krisher's Spite Fences.*

Public Awareness Announcement for Krisher's *Spite Fences*
Report Sack on Krisher's *Spite Fences*

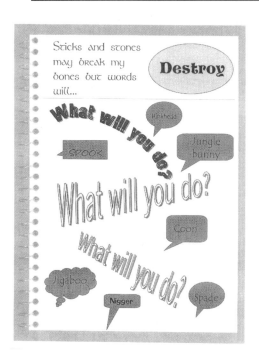 

Report Sack and Explanation

After reading the selected novel, ask students to brainstorm a list of personality traits exhibited by their main character. Then, ask them to find or construct at least five objects that represent the character's personality. They need to put the items in a brown paper lunch sack and write a one-page, typewritten summary of the book. The report sack is then shared with the class. See Lyn Bruner's *PowerPoint Presentation of Report Sack on Krisher's Spite Fences.*

Story Portrait and Explanation

This activity will help students make sense of their story and require them to display their understanding in a one-page graphic design. Ask students to begin by drawing a border around their "portrait" that is significant. Inside the border (in the "portrait" area), ask students to draw the big idea that they believe is the main idea or message of the story. Somewhere within the "portrait," ask them to write the theme of the work, in their own words. (What is the author's message, the big idea, or the moral of the story?) Somewhere else on the "portrait", ask them to write a quotation from the story that shows the big idea. In a one-page, typewritten paper, students should give a brief summary of the book that includes significant details and an explanation of their choices.

Timeline and Explanation

Ask students to recreate the journey of the hero/heroine or issue presented in their novel. They should use symbols, graphics, and text to show a sequence of events or ideas that develop the main theme of the novel.

Wanted Poster and Explanation

Using text, symbols, and quotes, ask students to design a poster that describes the person/character wanted by the law.

Performance-Based Assessment

To assess this project, use the *Assessment Rubric for PowerPoint or Hyperstudio Presentations* on page 58 and the *Cyber Journal Assessment Rubric* on page 59.

Bibliography

Gardner, H. (1983). *Frames of mind: The theory of multiple intelligences.* New York: Basic Books.

Krisher, T. (1999). *Spite fences.* New York: Econo-Clad Books.

Assessment Rubric for PowerPoint or Hyperstudio Presentations

	Exemplary	*Accomplished*	*Developing*	*Beginning*
Organization	Information presented in logical, interesting sequence	Information in logical sequence	Difficult to follow presentation, student jumps around	Cannot understand presentation, no sequence of information
Subject Knowledge	Demonstrates full knowledge by answering all class questions with explanations and elaborations	At ease with expected answers to questions but does not elaborate	Uncomfortable with information and is able to answer only rudimentary questions	Does not grasp information; cannot answer questions about subject
Graphics	Explain and reinforce screen text and presentation	Relate to text and presentation	Occasionally uses graphics that rarely support text and presentation	Uses superfluous graphics or no graphics
Research	Uses a variety of sources in reaching accurate conclusions	Uses a variety of sources in reaching conclusions	Presents only evidence that supports a preconceived point of view	Does not justify conclusions with research evidence
Screen Design	Includes variety of graphics, text, and animation that exhibits sense of wholeness. Creative use of navigational tools and buttons	Includes a variety of graphics, text and animation. Adequate navigational tools and buttons	Includes combinations of graphics and text, but buttons are difficult to navigate. Some buttons and navigational tools work	Either confusing or cluttered, barren or stark. Buttons or navigational tools are absent or confusing
Elocution/ Eye Contact	Maintains eye contact with precise pronunciation of terms and all audience members can hear	Maintains eye contact most of the time, pronouncing most words correctly. Most members can hear presentation	Occasionally uses eye contact, mostly reading presentation, and incorrectly pronounces terms with audience having difficulty hearing	Reads with no eye contact and incorrectly pronounces terms, speaking too quietly.

Cyber Journal Assessment Rubric

	Awesome	*Admirable*	*Acceptable*	*Attempted*
Introduction to Buddy	Friendly, inviting, descriptive e-mail introducing self and book.	Descriptive and inviting and addresses the book being shared	"Hi, my name is..." "I am a student at... in the..."	Minimal attempt to establish a relationship
Content of E-mail Entries	Insightful discussion of each chapter	Discussion is insightful but limited to major parts of the text	Generic and/or surface level comments	Inadequate discussion of the story
Active Responding to E-mail and Projects	Asked questions, made predictions, clarified information, critiqued buddy's projects	Comments addressed issues and projects shared with buddy	Commented on buddy's e-mail but didn't ask further questions or lend insight	Failed to acknowledge buddy's entries
Overall PowerPoint Slide Presentation	High technical accomplishments such as animation, timing, sound effects, text, graphics, color, use of space	Text represented by graphics and some use of animation and/or sound	Minimal use of graphics, sound, little or no animation, mostly textual	Inadequate presentation of key ideas of the story or social justice issue
MI Projects in PowerPoint	Shows insight, research into the social justice issue using a multiple intelligences approach	Good understanding of social justice issue shown through several of the multiple intelligences	Social justice issue not clearly defined. Limited by retelling the story and limited appeal to the multiple intelligences	Not much information about the story or issue. No appeal to the multiple intelligences
Book Review	Addresses literary quality, reader interest, potential popularity, and what the book is teaching (i.e., social and political philosophy)	Excellent summary with editorial comments. Some knowledge of reader interests	Personal opinion about "Why I liked/disliked this book." Brief summary of the book	Inadequate discussion of the ideas in the book or evaluation of it
Self-Reflection	Reflects on strengths and problems of the experience, as well as sets goals for the future. Discusses the buddy's insights and projects	Main focus of the reflective experience is based on project completed. Doesn't indicate future goals or insights	Descriptive as opposed to reflective. Limited to "I liked or disliked this project because..."	Not enough discussion to determine the value of this project

6

DRINKING AND DRIVING: A PORTFOLIO OF SOLUTIONS

Carolyn Suttles

*You can discover more about a person in an hour
of play than in a year of conversation.*

Plato

Overview of Authentic Learning

Students are asked to create a variety of products in response to this unit based on the Cynthia Voigt novel, *Izzy Willy-Nilly* and Internet research. Students include copies of partner e-mail discussions about the novel, a letter to a potential employer, Internet Web site evaluations, a survey and its results compiled in a graphic organizer, a PowerPoint presentation based on research, and a letter to a legislator. Through this portfolio, students not only show a deeper understanding of people living with disabilities but also learn strategies for creating a forum for discussion and for enacting changes in society.

NCTE/IRA Standards

This unit has students reading, writing, researching, and creating a presentation. They will be using the information garnered to take an informed stand on a social issue and to realize that action or inaction on their parts can affect culture (NCTE/IRA Standard #2). The students will also use various methods, such as peer discussion, writing letters to potential employers, and creating a presentation, to understand the novel they read and the research they conduct (NCTE/IRA Standard #3). These authentic assessments will also have a variety of audiences so that the connection is made between the performance and the audience (NCTE/IRA Standard #4). Because the students will be writing different pieces, they will learn strategies that are effective for various purposes (NCTE/IRA Standard #5). Finally, students conduct research, using technology to examine a social issue (NCTE/IRA Standards #7 and #8).

Materials

- ♦ Students each need a copy of the novel, *Izzy, Willy-Nilly* by Cynthia Voigt.
- ♦ Students each need access to e-mail and the Internet.

Planned Performance Tasks

E-mail Partners Discussing the Novel

"What do you think about what you have read thus far? Does the novel evoke any reaction on a personal level about the subject or characters? What do you like or dislike so far?"

Questions such as these are asked to begin the e-mail discussion between partners. Students should e-mail discussion and responses to the novel at least five times during the reading of the novel. Issues to be discussed are determined by the partners. Copies of the discussions are turned in to the teacher. (See *Excerpt from Instant Messaging* (between Tiffany Hinkle and Sara Rogers) and *Checklist Rubric to Assess the Peer Partner E-mail Discussion* on page 63.)

Excerpt from Instant Messaging (E-mail Partners)

TOS917: I like how Izzy compared herself to getting a makeover because in actuality, she did get one. Just hers was on the inside instead of on the out.

SRG904: Yeah, that's true. I wish the author would have written a little thing about what happened to Izzy after all of this.

TOS917: Yeah, like how they do in movies where they say how so and so went on to do this and so and so went on to do that. I would have liked that. I wonder what happened to Marco too?

SRG904: It's kind of funny how Izzy's mom and Rosamunde like each other...but then they don't.

TOS917: Yeah that is kind of funny.

SRG904: They constantly criticize each other because I think they both kind of think they know what is best for Izzy, but in reality, they are both helping her in different ways.

TOS917: Yeah, I agree, even though I don't really get why Rosamunde dislikes Izzy's mom so much.

SRG904: I think Rosamunde doesn't like Izzy's mom because she thinks she is kind of stuck up, but then again, she kind of is.

TOS917: She wants the best for Izzy and is protecting her, but Rosamunde wants the best for Izzy but instead of protecting her is making her face her fears.

SRG904: Yeah, her mom needs to look at all the good she has done for Izzy…even though Izzy is a strong person, I don't think she could have handled this on her own. It was too much.

TOS917: I was so glad when Izzy finally stood up to Marco.

SRG904: Me, too. Serves him right!! I'll be nice and call him a jerk for now, even though that's not my actual opinion. Georgie seems like she'd be a nice person. It's kind of ironic how Izzy never really gave her much thought before and in the end she kind of envied her.

TOS917: Yeah. Hey, I know what will happen to Marco after the novel ends. He probably dies from drunk driving.

SRG904: Or else he probably dies from Izzy's brothers beating him to a pulp.

TOS917: Yeah, for real. Gotta go. Talk to you later.

SRG904: See ya.

Checklist Rubric to Assess the
Peer Partner E-mail Discussion

Trait *Yes* *No*

Student planned a time schedule for the novel and e-mail discussion.

Student promptly replied to e-mail.

Student discussed characters in the novel and their character traits.

Student discussed the major theme and social issues in the novel.

Student discussed the literary elements.

Student discussed plot.

Student discussed characters' feelings at various stages in the novel.

Persuasive Letter of Application to an Employer

"Select a disability that you have interest in researching further. What types of limitations does a person with this disability have? What types of modifications, if any, would a person with this disability need in order to be a productive employee?" After researching this disability, each of you will write a letter to a prospective employer convincing that person to hire you. You should include those of your assets that would make you a good employee, but you should also mention any special modifications you would need to work at that job. (See *Sample Letter of Application* and *Assessment Rubric for Letter of Application* on page 66.) Criteria for the rubric were adapted from Markel (1992), *Technical Writing: Situations and Strategies*.

Sample Letter of Application

1046 Champion Lane
Warren, OH 44472
February 20, 2001

St. Joseph's Hospital
Ms. Rebecca Smith, Director of Personnel
530 East Lake Dr.
Warren, OH 44472

Dear Ms. Smith:

I am writing in reply to your ad in the Youngstown Vindicator for an accounting clerk. My high school course work was primarily in business and accounting, in which I held an A average. I received an associate's degree in accounting from Kent State University, Trumbull Campus, this past December, graduating with a 4.0. During my training, I inserviced at Heather Hills Nursing Home and ProLabs, so I am also familiar with medical terminology. Additionally, I am able to type 65 wpm and am proficient at American Sign Language and reading lips, as I am hearing impaired myself.

Being a large service and health-oriented employer, I am sure you are cognizant of the financial benefits to hiring a handicapped individual. There may be some modifications needed in my hiring, if you do not already have them available. Access to a TTY (teletypewriter) system and telephone with a flashing light, additional lighting for proper lip reading, a digital vibrating pager with read-out for in-house messages,, a fax machine, and a computer with modem access for any needed e-mails would be advantageous to our working relationship. I am certain that your facility already has specially designed fire/safety alarms installed.

Please contact me at your earliest convenience for a personal interview. I have enclosed my resume with vital information. I believe that my schooling, background, and initiative make me a viable candidate for your employment consideration, and I am eagerly anticipating our future business association.

Sincerely,
Shannon L. Burchett

Creating Surveys

"What type of questions would you put on a survey to obtain responses that could be compiled to inform your peers about the dangers of underage drinking and/or drinking and driving?" In groups of four, create surveys to be distributed to your peers about underage drinking and driving. The results will be compiled and displayed in a graphic organizer to ease the understanding of the results. The results will also be used later in this unit in a presentation. See *Teen Survey Questions* submitted by Shannon Burchett, Jessica Hudson, Missy Fink, and Brian Muresan.

Teen Survey Questions

1. How old are you?

2. Do you have your driver's license?

3. When do you drink alcohol?

4. Why do you drink?

5. If you don't drink, what keeps you from drinking?

6. How many drinks have you had in the past month?

7. How are you influenced to drink?

8. How do you feel about drinking and driving?

9. Have you ever ridden with a driver who had been drinking?

10. If you have, why did you do so?

11. On a scale from 1 to 10 with 1 being never and 10 being daily, how often do you drink?

12. How much do you drink at one time?

13. Do you drink alone?

Assessment Rubric for Letter of Application

	Excellent	*Acceptable*	*Not Yet*
Introductory paragraph	Identifies the source of information about the job; gives specifics of the ad or person; identifies the position you are interested in; states that you wish to be considered for the job; forecasts the rest of the letter.	Identifies the source of information, but lacks details; mentions the position desired, but not the exact title; mentions the job desired, but does not forecast the rest of the letter.	Does not mention the source of information about the job; vague description of the job desired; vague forecast of the rest of the letter.
Education paragraph	Strong topic sentence that forecasts the rest of the paragraph; uses considerable detail to develop the main idea.	Topic sentence gives a main idea and there are substantial details to support it.	Topic sentence is nondirectional and the paragraph fails to communicate your educational qualifications.
Employment paragraph	Begins with a topic sentence and elaborates a single idea; carefully defines duties for each position.	Topic sentence is descriptive and duties for each position are mentioned, but not detailed.	Topic sentence is too ambiguous and the paragraph fails to communicate your employment history.
Concluding paragraph	Compels action from the employer; refers to resume; requests an interview; gives your phone number.	Concluding paragraph stimulates action and gives general information about your credentials.	Concluding paragraph contains general information, but needs more details.
Appearance	Error-free and professional looking: adequate margins, clear and uniform type, no strikeovers or broken letters, 20 lb. paper; dark print.	Error-free and correctly formatted; even type and print; recycled paper.	Errors are distracting; poor print cartridge, wrinkled paper.

Evaluate Web Sites

"What characteristics can you use to determine if a website is reliable? What characteristics may be suspect, showing that a site is unreliable or prejudiced?" Using three teacher-selected URL's (any three, as long as one is a reliable primary source, one a secondary source, and one an unreliable, prejudiced source), each of you will evaluate the three Web sites using the evaluation form provided. After evaluating each of the sites, write a paragraph or two explaining the characteristics that you found to show reliability and those that showed unreliablility. See *Criteria to Evaluate a Web Site.*

Criteria to Evaluate a Web Site

Evaluating Web Resources

http:/www.library.kent.edu/internet/criteria.html

- Authority: Who created the site?

- Purpose and intended audience: Is the purpose and intention clear, including any bias or particular viewpoint?

- Accuracy and quality: Are facts documented and links provided to other quality Web resources?

- Currency: Is the information current and is the last update indicated?

- Usability: Is the site well-designed and stable?

State Research

"Which states have the best laws enforcing drinking and driving laws? Which states have the best education programs to deter drinking and driving and/or underage drinking? What types of programs are in place in other states to deter underage drinking?" Each of you will select one of the 50 states to research. Once you have found enough information about that state's deterrent and educational programs, you will meet back with the same groups of four that you were in to create the surveys. Each of you will contribute the information that you have found. Then your group will come to a consensus as to what you believe is the best solution to deter drinking and driving and underage drinking. You may mix and match programs and laws from the various states to create the combination of programs that would work best in your eyes.

Once your solution has been determined, you will create a PowerPoint Presentation to explain your program to the class. (See *Assessment Rubric for (Izzy, Willy, Nilly) PowerPoint Presentations or Hyperstudio Presentations* on page 68.)

Assessment Rubric for (*Izzy, Willy, Nilly*) PowerPoint Presentations or Hyperstudio Presentations

	1 points	*2 points*	*3 points*
layout design	very little design variation	some variation	creative designs keeps viewer's attention
use of color	difficult to read	easy to read but distracting	easy to view and creative use of color
size	font and graphics mostly too small to read	font and graphics are usually readable	font and graphics easily viewed
transitions	movement between slides distracting	movement smooth and usually not distracting	smooth movement and enhancing
animation	no or limited animation very distracting	Some animation but somewhat distracting	animation enhancing
sounds	very distracting or limited sounds	somewhat distract-ing or average use	enhancing sounds add to presentation
proofreading	many grammatical flaws—distracting	some grammatical flaws—somewhat distracting	flaws not distracting to presentation, very few
graphics/ artwork	none or inappropriate	few or somewhat inappropriate	appropriate, enhancing
title/conclu-sion	no introduction and/or conclusion	introduction but limited conclusion	good introduction and conclusion
content	limited sources or # of cards required	adequate sources and minimum # of cards	Fully covered topic with effective sources and sufficient # of cards
oral presen-tation	simply read cards	added some oral information to card content	card presentation added to oral presentation
quality of in-formation	sketchy, disjointed	minimal, not necessarily related	related, relevant

Assessment Rubric for a Persuasive Letter

	Excellent	Acceptable	Not Yet
Problem	Opens with a hook to introduce the problem; grabs reader's attention	Creates a favorable impression, but not as dynamic as a hook	Does not grab the reader's attention
Discussion	The sell—convinces the audience with concrete, specific evidence of your research; well-organized presentation that is factual and informative	Convincing evidence from your research, but lacking in specifics and details; information is clear, accurate, and concise	Discussion is not convincing to make a change. Needs references to your research; supporting details lack accuracy
Solution/ Request for Action	Motivational—Compels the reader to action; promotes good will	The solution is feasible and there is a request for action, though not compelling	No clear solution is evident and no clear request for action
Conventions	Correct letter format, spelling, punctuation; professional appearance	Correct letter parts; Error-free, acceptable appearance	Incorrect letter parts and not error-free; messy appearance

E-mail a Persuasive Letter to a Legislator

"What law dealing with underage drinking or drinking and driving would you like to see changed, improved, or added in our state? Are there any programs that you found that would work well in our state?" E-mail one of our legislators explaining the law or program that you think would improve our state. (See *Assessment Rubric for a Persuasive Letter* on page 69.) Criteria for the rubric were taken from Mehlich and Smith-Worthington (1997), *Technical Writing for Success: A School-to-Work Approach*.

Bibliography

Markel, M. H. (1992). *Technical writing: Situations and strategies*. New York: Martin's Press.

Mehlich, S., & Smith-Worthington, D. (1997) *Technical writing for success: A school-to-work approach*. Cincinnati, OH: South-Western Educational Publishing.

Voigt, C. (1995). *Izzy, Willy, Nilly*. New York: Alladdin Paperbooks.

7

POETRY NOTEBOOK PORTFOLIO

Linda J. Rice

We must cultivate our garden.

Voltaire, from *Candide*

Overview of Authentic Learning

Recognized as a genre that allows its readers and writers to express other-wise elusive qualities, poetry invites students to explore vast aspects of them-selves and human nature at large. By reading a wide variety of poetry and writing on a daily basis, students will deepen their understanding of poetry, its unique ability to tell stories, express thoughts, and convey emotion. Because many students approach the study of poetry with a tentative attitude often voiced as "I can't write poetry," this portfolio begins with several nonthreat-ening, easily doable activities that send the message that "poetry is all around you" and "you can be a poet." Daily writing prompts expose students to vari-ous resources of inspiration and provide them with a battery of ideas to develop into poems. Additionally, the portfolio's emphasis on daily writing establishes the connection between writing frequency and the improvement of ideas and skill. As students gain an understanding of, and ability to recognize and utilize, various literary terms and techniques, the portfolio components become more challenging. Students learn about and write poetic forms as concise as the haiku and as complex as the sestina. The overall portfolio, therefore, demonstrates students' development as writers, critical thinkers, and users of complex, often highly symbolic, literary strategies. Naturally, the teacher should present an ongoing and diverse array of "good" poetry from a variety of cultures and literary traditions so that students gain a broad exposure to the open, expansive nature of the genre. The teacher should also promote discussion and analysis of what makes a poem "good" or "effective," and in doing so encourage students to both recognize and apply these qualities to their own writing. Writer's workshop is recommended as a forum to help students elicit additional feedback on their work. In this forum, students share drafts of their work with peers who offer additional feedback. By sharing ideas and having opportunities to revise, students expand poetic possibilities and build stronger works for the portfolio. And, having a collection of drafts enables students to see their development as writers.

NCTE/IRA Standards

In this unit, students will:

♦ Respond daily to a wide range of print and nonprint texts (NCTE/IRA Standard #1) as a means of gathering ideas to develop into full works for their Poetry Portfolio. In responding to these daily writing prompts, students will periodically need to draw on their prior experience (NCTE/IRA Standard #3). The primary focus of the daily prompts is for students to gain a battery of possibilities for their writing-both by extending content and viewing varied forms and models, thus serving to model the "brainstorming" or exploratory component of the writing process (NCTE/IRA Standard #5). Some prompts will require students to utilize or interpret figurative language (NCTE/IRA Standard #6), whereas others will encourage students to understand diverse language patterns from other cultures (NCTE/IRA Standard #9). In this initial idea-building and filing stage of writing, students will often be encouraged to utilize their reflective and creative skills (NCTE/IRA Standard #11) to extend the prompts into personally meaningful and enjoyable outlets for expression.

♦ Compose five different forms of Japanese poetry and find accompanying artwork to illustrate key ideas present in their own writing (NCTE/IRA Standard #12). In conjunction with this portion of the portfolio, students will study characteristics of Japanese culture through a variety of print and nonprint texts from the school's library/media center (NCTE/IRA Standards #1 & #7). Although the highly structured nature of the Japanese forms for this unit (haiku, renga, tanka, dodoitsu, and sedoka) require students to apply knowledge of language structure, use, and patterns from another culture (NCTE/IRA Standards #6 & #9), their freedom to seek and/or create matching visuals draws on their creative skill in the class's literary community (NCTE/IRA Standard #11).

♦ Compose a variety of poems that specify strict guidelines, including line count, rhyme scheme, syllable count, refrain, repetition, and figurative language (NCTE/IRA Standards #3, #6, & #12). Self revision and peer revision will be integral for each written work required as a part of the portfolio, thus giving students opportunities to seek and hear input and perspectives from others to promote writing as a process, rather than product only (NCTE/IRA Standard #5). In the writer's workshop community, students participate as knowledgeable, reflective, creative, and critical members (NCTE/IRA Standard #11).

Performance Tasks

Performance Task for Daily Writing Prompts

In order to help students envision, develop, and maintain a range of ideas for their own writing, daily writing prompts are a routine part of developing the Poetry Portfolio. During the course of the poetry unit (which can easily span a nine-week grading period on the traditional schedule) the teacher will provide a quote, statement, question, work of literature, film clip, song, work of art, etc. (see suggestions in the *Sample Writing Prompts* on page 74) to which students will respond in writing. Ideally, students will have 5 to 10 minutes to reflect on the prompt in writing. On some days, they will wish for more time, whereas on other days, they may be frustrated at having little to write about the topic; that is normal. Each of the daily prompts is to be dated and kept in the student's Poetry Portfolio for future consideration and possible development into a feature poem for the final portfolio. This keeps students writing on a daily basis and provides some starters for days the class has writer's workshop. Over time, when daily writing becomes a routine part of class meetings, students' writing fluency and sustained focus on a single theme, story, or concept increases. This is the trend for which students should strive. See *Assessment Rubric for Daily Writing Prompts* on page 75.

Japanese Poetic Forms

Name	*Line arrangement and syllable count*
Haiku	5-7-5
Dodoitsu	7-7-7-5
Tanka	5-7-5-7-7
Renga (tanka in series; linked form)	5-7-5-7-7, 5-7-5-7-7, etc.
Sedoka	5-7-7-5-7-7

Sample Writing Prompts

Quotes, Poems, and Topics for Reflection

"It's about gaining control of your life and letting go at the same time." *Tin Cup*, Kevin Costner

"Someone, somewhere will say _____ was here." *Evening Star*
(fill in your name)

"Your life has been my life." *Evening Star*, Marion Ross

"I have always felt the need to go on, especially when the world around me seems to have stopped." *Evening Star, Shirley McClain*

"The deepest feeling always shows itself in silence-not in silence, but restraint. *Silence*, Marianne Moore

"I loved my friend," poem by Langston Hughes

Whether we see things as good or bad depends on our perspective. (use as introduction to *Triolet, First Photos of a Flu Virus,* by Harold Witt)

"Too hard it is to sing/In these untuneful times!" (use as introduction to Rondel) Austin Dobson

"Time will say nothing but I told you so…" or "If I could tell you I would let you know…" W. H. Auden (use as introduction to Villanelle)

Two perspectives in an argument or when you need to be alone and when you need to be with others (use as introduction to Pantoum, *Iva's Pantoum,* by Marilyn Hacker)

Compulsive subjects, obsessions, dream states (use as introduction for Sestina)

Pictures and Famous Works of Art

Yearbooks

Students' own photos

Old calendars

Transparencies projected for whole-class to view together

Film Clips

The Long Walk Home (last 15 minutes, breaking up the car pool)

The Mirror Has Two Faces (scene where Barbara Streisand is giving a lecture on love)

Musical Selections

Note: The key here is to avoid "popular" music that the students already listen to since that often conjures up stereotypes and cliches. Instead, choose selections that are interesting and unusual. Jazz, classical, and celtic works such as the following seem to work well.

"Capim"by Manhattan Transfer (Brasil CD)

"O Fortuna" from Carmina Burana by Carl Orff (1895–1982) and other dramatic selections from Summon the Heroes, John Williams' conducting the Boston Pops Orchestra with music to celebrate the Olympic Centennial

Exile by Enya (Watermark CD)

Assessment Rubric for Daily Writing Prompts

Mature	*Emerging*	*Novice*
Demonstrates effort to respond thoughtfully and/or creatively; shows self-direction and fluency	May show an energetic start, but then fades to loss of ideas and associations needed to write fluidly for the allotted time	Brief responses and/or choppy series of starters that lack sustained engagement and connective reasoning

Performance Task for Japanese Poetic Forms and Accompanying Artwork

Before having their students write any Japanese poetic forms (see *Japanese Poetic Forms* on page 73), teachers will likely want to take advantage of the opportunity to expose students to this unique culture. A trip to the media center to find books and facts on the Japanese people, their country, customs, values, and literature, would certainly help students to situate this form in a context beyond syllable counts. Also, with a basic understanding of Japanese culture, students may properly mirror some of the styles and subjects traditional to Japanese poets such as nature, reflection, and change. After facilitating students' exploration of Japanese culture, the teacher will introduce the five poetic forms, making sure that students understand how to count syllables. Works of art (hard copies or on transparencies or PowerPoint) serve as an especially good prompt because they provide students with visual stimulation to be captured in words. Although teachers are certainly welcome to pick and choose from among the five forms, they should be mindful of the order in which the forms are presented. Beginning with the haiku is advantageous because students will have had practice with the 5-7-5 syllable sequencing before advancing to the tanka, that builds on the haiku with its 5-7-5-7-7 format. After writing several of each of the Japanese forms (see examples, presented in *Sample Japanese Poetic Forms* on page 76), students take time to pick favorites, conference with peers, revise as desired, and then begin designing and/or selecting graphics that capture the spirit of their writing. The artistic works should be intermingled with poems to form an aesthetically pleasing layout merging form and function (see examples, *Sample Tanka* on page 77 and *Sample Dodoitsu* on page 77). See *Assessment Rubric for Japanese Forms and Accompanying Artwork* on page 78.

Sample Japanese Poetic Forms (by Kyle Stefano)

Haiku	*Mother Nature* (this appeared under a photograph of a mountain range reflected in a pond) Perfect symmetry. Mother Nature shows power that stems from beauty.
Renga	*Center* (this appeared with a photograph of a sunflower) The center is strong Tiny specks, like citizens making a town whole Centers are always needed for water, and food, and life Bunches of pilgrims, stunningly smooth in yellow, grown from the center. Centers give their own beauty to the outside for judgment. Sometimes the beauty is plucked straight from its maker, for no good reason. A larger life form yearning for beauty between his hands.
Tanka	See Sample Tanka ("Your Voice") with graphic.
Dodoitsu	See Sample Dodoitsu ("Tears") with graphic.
Sedoka	*Frightened Petals* (this appeared in the middle of a picture of two long stem roses with open petals) Radiant flower, With your scent gracing Heaven. Why do petals close at night? Darkness can't hurt you. Wake up with the shining sun, Your beauty waits for the light.

Sample Tanka (by Kyle Stefano)
Sample Dodoitsu (by Kyle Stefano)

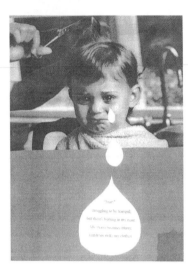

Your Voice

Hearing your voice speak
Is like listening to rain
Tap on my window.
Both assure me much comfort
after bad days and bad dreams.

Tears

Struggling to be tranquil,
But there's burning in my nose.
My vision becomes blurry,
Teardrops strike my clothes.

Performance Task for Specialized/ Technical Poetic Forms

After students have grown accustomed to syllable count through the five Japanese forms, they are ready to embark on the most rigorous portion of the unit intended to stretch their Poetry Portfolio to the limit. Although teachers are certainly welcome to pick and choose from the six Specialized/Technical Poetic Forms (see *Triolet Guidelines* on page 79, *Sample Triolet* on page 79, *Rondel Guidelines* on page 80, *Sample Rondel* on page 80, *Rondeau Guidelines* on page 81, *Sample Rondeau* on page 81, *Villanelle Guidelines* on page 82, *Sample Villanelle on page 82*, *Pantoum Guidelines* on page 83, *Sample Pantoum* on page 83, *Sestina Guidelines* on page 84, and *Sample Sestina* on page 85 for guidelines and examples) overviewed in this chapter, it is very important to consider sequencing. The Pantoum and Sestina are notably more difficult and challenging for students to write than are the Triolet, Rondeau, and Rondel; therefore, it is highly recommended that at least two of these three forms be included in the students' portfolios before conquering the prior. Teachers can assist students' effort to get started on these forms by choosing daily writing prompts that align well with the example poems. Recommended subjects are provided in the *Pantoum* (page 83) and *Sestina* guidelines (page 84); also see *Sample Writing Prompts* on page 74. As students work through any of these Specialized/Technical Poetic Forms,

Assessment Rubric for Japanese
Forms and Accompanying Artwork

Applicable Forms	Exceptional	Acceptable	Needs Improvement
Haiku Renga Tanka Dodoitsu Sedoka	• Precise adherence to overall form/syllable count • Sustains theme/idea throughout • Exemplifies efficiency of form-every word counts!	Exhibits one of the following problems: • Error in syllable or line count (does not adhere to form) • Lacks cohesive theme or shifts from one topic to another without a compelling/poetic reason or purpose • Weak word choice(s) that takes away from maximum efficiency of Japanese poetic form	Exhibits two or more of the following problems: • Error in syllable or line count (does not adhere to form) • Lacks cohesive theme or shifts from one topic to another without a compelling/poetic reason or purpose • Weak word choice(s) that takes away from maximum efficiency of Japanese poetic form

Artistic Component	Exceptional	Acceptable	Needs Improvement
Relevance	Precise link or exemplification of content or image found in the poem	Establishes link between poem and visual but in a simplistic manner such as an advertisement from a magazine	Weak correlation between poem and visual
Layout	Provides thoughtful balance/integration of poem and art or meaningful juxtaposition	Basic layout (poem-picture-poem-picture) that lacks creative thought and/or integration	Artwork appears as an appendix after the poems or is not clearly laid out to parallel poem it is intended to accompany
Implementation	Neat and colorful use of media that will not smear; easily readable and demonstrates careful, thoughtful investment of time and effort	Neat and colorful overall, but fairly basic without a clear demonstration of superior artistry or investment of time and effort	Lacking in neatness; somewhat haphazard with no compelling artistic appeal

they will benefit from multiple opportunities to engage in writer's workshop where they can share their ideas and elicit feedback from peers. When mindful of the rubrics for each form, teachers can build in more than just strict adherence to form (line count, rhyme scheme, etc.) and incorporate figurative language and a vast array of literary techniques that help poetry come to life.

After students have completed their individual Poetry Portfolios for this unit, the teacher may want to encourage each to select a "favorite" original composition for a class booklet. This offers a nice note of closure to the unit and provides an audience for sharing "best works."

Triolet Guidelines

Helpful Tidbit	Lyric form—originally a form sung to the accompaniment of the lyre (stringed instrument from Greek culture) or other musical instrument
Specifications	Octave (8-line stanza)
	Rhymes abaaabab
	Line 1 repeats as line 4 & 7
	Line 2 repeats as line 8, last line of poem
	Sometimes written as two stanzas, a quintet (5-line stanza) followed by a triplet (3-line stanza)
Examples	Harold Witt (1923–) "First Photos of Flu Virus"
	Barbara Howes (1914–) "Early Supper"—this example skillfully triples the triolet form

Sample Triolet

The Roses
By: Kyle Stefano

Bending down to experience the roses,	a (line 1)
drawing in a gulp of air,	b (line 2)
The wild petals tickle our noses,	a
bending down to experience the roses.	a (line 4 repeats line 1)
The flowers stand there, bloomed in poses	a
giving us no option, but to share,	b
bending down to experience the roses	a (line 7 repeats lines 1 & 4)
drawing in a gulp of air.	b (line 8 repeats line 2)

Rondel Guidelines

Helpful Tidbit   Lyric form—originally a form sung to the accompaniment of the lyre (stringed instrument from Greek culture) or other musical instrument

Specifications
- Can be 13 or 14 lines
- If 13 lines, consists of two quatrains (4-line stanzas) followed by a quintet (5-line stanza)
- If 14 lines, consists of two quatrains (4-line stanzas) followed by a sestet (6-line stanza)
- Line 1 repeats as line 7
- Line 2 repeats as line 8
- Lines 1 & 2 close the poem (either lines 12 & 13 or lines 13 & 14 depending on which form is chosen)

The rhyme scheme is as follows:
- Stanza 1 (quartet), abab
- Stanza 2 (quartet), abba
- Stanza 3 (quintet or sestet), abbab or abab

Example   Austin Dobson (1840–1921) "Too Hard It Is To Sing"

Sample Rondel

My Angel
By: Kyle Stefano

Once again, my Angel saves me,	a	(line 1)
I shouldn't be surprised.	b	(line 2)
Guiding my life-how it should be,	a	
Watching me through mystic eyes.	b	
My guardian lifts me above all cries,	b	
Working in Eternity.	a	
Once again, my Angel saves me,	a	(line 7 repeats line 1)
I shouldn't be surprised.	b	(line 8 repeats line 2)
When my Angel is there, I can see	a	
The truth behind the lies.	b	
I never feel alone or empty,	a	
The presence I cannot deny.	b	
Once again, my Angel saves me,	a	(line 13 repeats lines 1 & 7)
shouldn't be surprised.	b	(line 14 repeats lines 2 & 8)

Rondeau Guidelines

Helpful Tidbit   Lyric form—originally a form sung to the accompaniment of the lyre (stringed instrument from Greek culture) or other musical instrument

Specifications   • 15-line poem

• Arranged in a quintet (5-line stanza), quatrain (4-line stanza), and sestet (6-line stanza)

• Each line has 8 syllables

• The first few words of line 1 act as a refrain in lines 9 and 15 (Note: The refrain lines do not rhyme, but repeating the fragment seems to imply the rest of the line, including the rhyme, so the rhyme acts invisibly).

The rhyme scheme is as follows:

• Stanza 1 (quintet), aabba

• Stanza 2 (quatrain), aabRefrain

• Stanza 3 (sestet), aabbaRefrain

Example   Barbara Howes (1914–) "Death of a Vermont Farm Woman"

Sample Rondeau

My Own Bathroom
By: Kyle Stefano

Do you think after all these years	a
I'll miss all your brotherly jeers?	a
The idea-my own bathroom sink!	b
Quiet time? I'm able to think!	b
Go ahead! Explore those careers!	a
Ah! You're gone! No more pulling ears	a
I've never gave so many cheers!	a
Wow-you left before I could blink,	b
After all these years?	Refrain
Now-I can't miss you-No more tears	a
From beatings from you and your peers!	a
Oddly I find my waste of ink,	b
Being only child really stinks.	b
I never thought I'd miss your leers	a
After all these years	Refrain

Villanelle Guidelines

History

- Originated in Italy in the 15th Century as a folk song
- Later used in England and France

Specifications

- 19 lines structured as 5 tercets (3-line stanzas) and a concluding quatrain (4-line stanza)
- Each tercet rhymes aba The quatrain rhymes abaa
- Line 1 repeats in lines 6 & 12 (ends of stanzas 2 & 4)
- Line 3 repeats in lines 9 & 15 (ends of stanzas 3 & 5)
- Line 3 is also repeated-but turns into a question-as the last line of the poem (final quatrain, line 19)
- There is no set metrical pattern (stressed and unstressed syllables), though lines are usually close to the same syllabic length.

Example   W.H. Auden (1907–1973) "If I Could Tell You"

Sample Villanelle

In My Dreams
By Kyle Stefano

Coloring my dreams tonight	a	(line 1)
will be things one never really sees,	b	
For it may be a scary sight!	a	(line 3)
Creatures making shadows in the light	a	
escorting martians from our TVs,	b	
Coloring my dreams tonight.	a	(line 6 repeats line 1)
A pea-brained fly taking a bite	a	
of an elephant throwing peanuts at me,	b	
For it may be a scary sight!	a	(line 9 repeats line 3)
All the leaves turn bright and white	a	
and people eat them off the trees,	b	
Coloring my dreams tonight.	a	(line 12 repeats lines 1 & 6)
In my underwear, I'm flying a kite	a	
in front of people drinking tea,	b	
For it may be a scary sight!	a	(line 15 repeats lines 3 & 9)
All the kids are always right	a	
and I'm this huge scary queen bee	b	
What will color my dreams tonight?	a	
May it be a scary sight?	a	(line 3 turns into a question in the last line of the poem)

Pantoum Guidelines

History and Information of Interest	• Malayan form popularized in the 15th Century, but with older roots in Chinese and Persian poetry. • Has a sound effect of chanting with excessive repetition • As a result of the pattern of repeating lines, the two subjects (woven together in the poem—could be people or conflicting ideas, concepts, or arguments) work their way down the poem in a back-and-forth, push-pull movement. • The poem may be thought of as a game of "Mother, May I?" where one of the instructions is to take two steps forward and one backward.
Specifications	• This form can have an indefinite number of quatrains (4-line stanzas) of any line length. • Lines 2 & 4 of each stanza become lines 1 & 3 of the following stanza. • At its close, the poem circles back to end where it began. The last line of the poem repeats the first line. • Line 2 of the final stanza repeats line 3 of stanza 1.
Recommended Subjects	• An argument between two people • 2 distinct perspectives
Example	Marilyn Hacker (1942–) "Iva's Pantoum"

Sample Pantoum

Battle of the Sexes
By: Kyle Stefano

The rivalry has always been there,   (line 1)
men think they're superior, women think they're best.   (line 2)
The grudge only makes the attraction stronger
but neither sex will submit to the other.   (line 4)

Men think they're superior, women think they're best.   (line 2 from previous stanza
Women gawk at men's rough hands and dirty nails,   becomes line 1 of subse-
but neither sex will submit to the others.   quent stanza throughout)
Men can't comprehend women's smooth feminine skin.   (line 4 from previous stanza
     becomes line 3 of subse-
     quent stanza throughout)

Women gawk at men's rough hands and dirty nails, but
mesmerized by their masculine shape.
Men can't comprehend women's smooth feminine shape,
but admire their mysterious gentle frame.

Mesmerized by their masculine shape,
the grudge only makes the attraction stronger.
Admiring their mysterious gentle frame,
The rivalry has always been there.   (line 1 is repeated as the last
     line of the poem)

Sestina Guidelines

Background and Some Interesting Information

- Originated in the 12th Century—a time in which mysticism and numerology were popular
- Form based on sixes (mystical number). Each word is positioned next to each other word twice in the course of the poem.
- If we make a hexagon of end words (called ABCDEF) and connect each end word to every other end word it touches, we see that the poem is indeed graphically complete.
- This creates a closed, web-like structure.

Specifications

- Six 6-line stanzas and a final tercet (3-line stanza)
- The last words in the first stanza are repeated as the last words in all subsequent stanzas, in a defined order.
- All six key words (end words of lines 1-6 in the poem) also appear in the tercet (3 as last words; 3 in the middle of each line)
- The last word of each stanza becomes the last word of the first line of the next stanza.
- The last word of the first line repeats as the last word of the poem.

The Pattern for Repeating Words is as follows:

- Stanza 1, ABCDEF
- Stanza 2, FAEBDC
- Stanza 3, CFDABE
- Stanza 4, ECBFAD
- Stanza 5, DEACFB
- Stanza 6, BDFECA
- Stanza 7, ECA (with BDF midline)

Recommended Subjects

- Subjects call for intricacy to fit the form.
- This is an especially good form for exploring compulsive subjects, problems without solutions, obsessions, or dream states.

Example

Frances Mayes, "Sestina for the Owl"

Sample Sestina

(Note pattern in which end words are repeated)

Protection from Bad Attitudes
By: Kyle Stefano

How do you see the glass? Half empty, half full?	A
For me it depends on my mood, but the second	B
I don't have a smile on my face	C
people call me a pessimist. I consider myself	D
to be a generally happy person because I'm uncomfortable	E
with other people's negative attitudes.	F
I often wonder what causes a person to give these attitudes,	F
these heavy attitudes that contaminate my mind full	A
of rancid words that weigh quite uncomfortably	E
on my center. My question that comes second	B
is why a pessimist chooses to spread his disease to me,	D
does he not appreciate the normal smile on my face?	C
For when I hear negativity, my vulnerable face	C
is not strong enough to protect a smile from bad attitudes.	F
As unfair as it may be, I find myself	D
unwillingly accepting these vibes that are full	A
of bitter feelings. It's not second-	B
hand smoke; only the smoker can protect me from being uncomfortable.	E
But the smoker does not care about my uncomfortable	E
position. He'll blow bundles of smoke into my face,	C
just like a pessimist will portray a bad vibe until the second	B
I adopt his bad attitude.	F
Does it make him feel more full	A
to know he doesn't share the anger by himself?	D
They'll realize his plot, and I wonder to myself	D
why I let such a petty person make me uncomfortable.	E
I know I'm capable of living a life full	A
of smiles and joy-but the test is to not let other faces	C
sculpt my own to match their droopy attitudes.	F
I must not conform, not for a second.	B
The way I save my soul, even only a second	B
after receiving bad news is I tell myself,	D
despite my problem or attitude,	F
someone else's situation is way more uncomfortable	E
than my own, and his face	C
is still high. My joy will leave me full.	A
So, now the second someone tries to leave me uncomfortable,	(B) E
I immediately tell myself to forget his face	(D) C
because my attitude shows me a glass that is half full.	(F) A

Assessment Rubric for Specialized/Technical Forms of Poetry

Applicable Forms	Exceptional	Acceptable	Needs Improvement
Triolet Rondel Rondeau Villanelle	Follows required number of lines completely	1 to 2 errors in line form	3 or more errors in line form
Triolet Rondel Rondeau Villanell	Follows required number of syllables	1 to 2 errors or overreliance on slant rhymes	3 or more errors
Pantoum Sestina	Topic works well (e.g., sestina is a good form for exploring compulsive subjects, problems without solutions, obsessions, or dream states)	Topic is loosely related or shifts-loses momentum or cohesion in the course of the poem	No deliberate connection with suggested topics to help form follow function
Triolet Rondel Rondeau Villanelle Pantoum Sestina	Lines (or words, as applicable) repeated where required	1 to 2 errors in repetition	3 or more errors in repetition
Considerations for all Specialized/ Technical Poetic Forms	*Exceptional*	*Acceptable*	*Needs Improvement*
Fluidity	Reads smoothly to indicate a strong sense of fluidity and awareness of sound quality	Mostly smooth, but some occurrences of imbalance	Largely inattentive to sound quality and poetic balance or reads more like prose than poetry
Clarity and development	Clearly, logically, and creatively developed in a way that creates a moment, conveys an emotion, or tells a story	Clear overall, but perhaps with noticeable side tracks or language that is heavy-handed or imprecise and causes the poem to lose focus	Abstraction to the point of distraction; as though only the writer can capture the meaning
Literary Techniques	Naturally integrates a variety of literary techniques to demonstrate how poetic language conveys meaning/feeling differently than prose	Employs a variety of literary techniques, but sometimes appearing to be more deliberate (as if to meet a requirement) than natural	Utilizes 2 or fewer literary techniques
Drafts and Evidence of Revision	2 drafts with evidence of self-revision and input from peer reader	Only 1 draft or 2 drafts without revisions noted or without input from peer reader	No drafts or evidence of conferencing or revising

Bibliography

Powell, D. (1981). *What can I write about? 7000 topics for high school students.* Urbana, IL: National Council of Teachers of English.

Rexroth, K. (1964). *One hundred poems from the Japanese.* New York: New Directions.

Movies

Harling, R. (Director). (1999). *Evening star* [Film]. Starring Shirley MacClaine and Bill Paxton. Paramount Studios.

Pearce, R. (Director). (1997). *The long walk home* [Film]. Starring Sissy Spacek and Whoopi Goldberg. Santa Monica, CA: Artisan Entertainment.

Shelton, R. (Director). (2001). *Tin cup* [Film]. Starring Kevin Costner and Rene Russo. Burbank, CA: Warner Studios.

Streisand, Barbara (Director). (2001). *The mirror has two faces* [Film]. Starring Barbara Streisand and Jeff Bridges. Culver City, CA: Columbia/Tristar.

Poems

Auden, W. H. (1945). *If I could tell you* [Online]. Available: http://recmusic.org/lieder/a/audent/a1.html.

Dobson, A. (1987). In F. Mayes. *The discovery of poetry.* San Diego: Harcourt Brace Jovanovich.

Hacker, M. (1980). In F. Mayes. *The discovery of poetry.* San Diego: Harcourt Brace Jovanovich.

Howes, B. (1959). In F. Mayes. *The discovery of poetry.* San Diego: Harcourt Brace Jovanovich.

Hughes, L. (1926). *Poems* (to F.S.). New York: Alfred A. Knopf.

Mayes, F. (1987). *The discovery of poetry.* San Diego: Harcourt Brace Jovanovich.

Witt, H. (1987). In F. Mayes. *The discovery of poetry.* San Diego: Harcourt Brace Jovanovich.

Music

Boston Pops Orchestra. John Williams. (1996) *O Fortuna. On Summon the heroes* [CD]. New York: Sony Classical.

Enya. (1988). *Exile.* On Watermark [CD]. Burbamk, CA: Wea/Warner Brothers.

Manhattan Transfer. (1990) *Capim.* On Brasil [CD]. New York: Atlantic.

8

PORTFOLIO FOR WRITING A SHORT STORY

Colleen Ruggieri

I think, therefore I am.

Decartes

Overview of Authentic Learning

Analytical ways of knowing are privileged in our Western culture. Even in a discipline such as English, devoted to stories and storytelling, narrative ways of knowing are rarely allowed as ways for students to express themselves. If narrative writing is permitted, all too often we turn students loose to write poetry or short stories without scaffolding the thinking process. The purpose of this assessment is to show students strategies to stimulate ideas, and plan plot and character development that will lead to writing a short story. If a short story is going to work, it must have the right ingredients. With the right materials and a good recipe, students can create some pleasant surprises. The student examples for this assessment were taken from the portfolio of Patrick Alexander from Boardman High School. Ideas for these activities were adapted from Crawford Kilian's (2001) *Advice on Novel Writing.*

NCTE/IRA Standards

In this assessment, students will:

◆ Create a storyboard for a short story. In doing so, students will employ a wide range of strategies as they write and use different writing process elements appropriately to communicate with different audiences for a variety of purposes (NCTE/IRA Standard #5).

◆ Construct a scene for a short story. In doing so, students will apply knowledge of language structure, language conventions, media techniques, figurative language, and genre to create texts (NCTE/IRA Standard #6).

◆ Develop a character resume and collage. In doing so, students will use spoken, written, and visual language to accomplish their own purposes (NCTE/IRA Standard #12).

◆ Compose a dialogue. In doing so, students will adjust their use of spoken, written, and visual language to communicate effectively with a variety of audiences and for different purposes (NCTE/IRA Standard #4), and students will employ a wide range of strategies as they write and use different writing process elements appropriately to communicate with different audiences for a variety of purposes (NCTE/IRA Standard #5).

◆ Write a short story. In doing so, students will adjust their use of spoken, written, and visual language to communicate effectively with a variety of audiences and for different purposes NCTE/IRA Standard #4); students will employ a wide range of strategies as they write and use different writing process elements appropriately to communicate with different audiences for a variety of purposes (NCTE/IRA Standard #5); students will apply knowledge of language structure, language conventions, media techniques, figurative language, and genre to create texts (NCTE/IRA Standard #6); students will participate as knowledgeable, reflective, creative, and critical members of a variety of literacy communities (NCTE/IRA Standard #11); and, students will use spoken, written, and visual language to accomplish their own purposes (NCTE/IRA Standard #12).

Performance Tasks for Portfolio

Storyboarding

Storyboarding usually means arranging a sequence of images for a film or commercial. But students can storyboard a short story, also, and it can be a helpful way to organize the plot. That's because we do not ordinarily think plot. We have an idea for a story (e.g., immigrant boy finds family dynasty in Nevada wilderness) and a random assortment of mental images (e.g., encounter with a grizzly bear, wild ride to rescue son from kidnappers, casino scene, etc). How do we get from these fragments to a coherent plot? Kilian suggests taking a stack of 3"x5" index cards and jotting down an image or scene on each one, just in the order the ideas occur to you. When you have five or ten or twenty such cards, lay them out in the sequence you envision for the story. You certainly don't have a card for each scene in the short story, but you have the scenes that your subconscious seems to deal with. You also have numerous gaps to fill. That means more cards as you think of new ideas. Maybe some of the new ideas are better than the original ones, so some of the old cards go in the trash. New characters emerge to fulfill functions in the story, so you create even more cards. Once you have at least the main sequence of events clearly mapped out on your cards, you can begin to transfer them to a more manageable synopsis or outline. So, let's get started! See Patrick's Storyboarding for *"Mama's Boy"*.

Storyboarding for "Mama's Boy"

Armed intruders threaten A.C. and hold his mother at gunpoint	"I am a mama's boy": A.C. blames himself for his mother's murder	"Nobody knows that I'm a mama's boy no more": A.C. decides to change who he is to avoid ridicule and win back his destroyed reputation	A.C. vandalizes school property to show he's a man	A.C. steals to show he's a man	A.C. plans revenge with his friends to show he's a man
Nightmares provoke him to take further action	"Vengeance is mine": A.C. finally decides to kill his mother's murderer	A.C. neglects grave warnings of friends and his pastor/father	A.C. provokes friends to scout out the killer	Bumps into woman and spills the groceries she carries	A.C. falls for flattery, but finally reaches realization as to what it means to be a man

Constructing a Scene

Constructing a scene is the basic unit of fiction, not the sentence or the paragraph. According to Killian, every scene in a story has both verbal and nonverbal content. The verbal content may be a young man fervently courting a girl. The nonverbal content appears in the way you present the scene: You want your reader to think that the young man is touchingly awkward, or obnoxiously crude. In effect, you are like an attorney presenting a case to the jury. You show the awkward behavior: "Aw, the poor lunk!"—then the scene has succeeded. Every scene presents a problem of some kind for one or more of the characters, and shows us how the characters deal with that problem. That, in turn, shows us something about the characters and moves the story ahead. Ask students to take one of their cards and construct the scene. See a *Constructed Scene* by Patrick Alexander.

Constructed Scene

Then, from my seat in the kitchen where I'd been daydreaming, I heard a rush of footsteps, a heavy knock on our front door, and three quick rings on our doorbell. Before I could jump up from the dinner table to answer it, the front door flew open. Mama, her apron wrapped around her waist and rollers in her silky hair, calmly approached the entrance as I looked on in sheer disbelief. Our intruders, armed and motionless, stood before us in the doorway. There were two of them, their dark faces covered by ski masks. The bigger one sauntered in front of the other and shoved me against the wall.

"What you lookin' at, son? You 'fraid? Big as you is, ain't you gonna get the door fo' yo' mama?" he questioned.

Before I could choke out a response, he threw back his head, howling at the thought of a scornful reply of his own.

"Oh, forgive me, Shorty," he snarled between a series of snickers, "I done forgot already! You da mama's boy everyone 'round da 'hood be talking about, ain't you?"

I swallowed hard, but I don't remember responding to anything he said. In fact, I don't remember anything else happening until the second intruder suddenly came out of his stationary position at the doorway and held Mama at gunpoint. He kept repeating something in a high, squeaky voice, but I could not hear what he was saying. Seconds later, amid her helpless cries for mercy, he pulled the trigger, spraying her with a steady storm of bullets. The ear-splitting shots rang out until, hearing the whine of police sirens, he headed for the door. He paused momentarily, deciding what to say to me.

"Look here, you little mama's boy," he wailed, "if you say anything about this, I'll kill you too!" Content with these parting words, he darted out the door.

Character Resume: Short Story Brainstorming for Protagonist

One useful way to learn more about your characters is to fill out a "resume" for them. The information included in Patrick's resume provides an example of information that Kilian suggests we consider. See the Character Resume for Adrian Christopher Dawson, a resume created by Patrick Alexander for his main character. Although students may not include all this information in their stories, visualizing their character in this way will prepare them to develop their characters through action and dialogue when the time comes. If time permits, ask students to make a collage of images from magazines, clip art, or the Internet to further visualize their character's personality and interests. They should understand their characters well enough to give the characters adequate motivation for their actions and words. They can then develop the plot as a series of increasingly serious problems. Solutions to the problems must be appropriate to the characters.

Character Resume for Adrian Christopher Dawson

Male/Female: Male character

Name: Adrian Christopher Dawson

Nickname: A.C.

Address: 666 13th Avenue, Philadelphia, PA

Phone Number: N/A

Date/Place of Birth: October 13th, 1983/Philadelphia, PA

Physical Description: Tall and slightly built (6'0", 165 lbs.), black braided hair, dark brown eyes, mahogany-colored skin, long thin sideburns, dragon tattoos on both arms

Family: Lives with father and no siblings, mother recently passed away

Hobbies/Interests: Writing in his journal, fixing cars, hanging out with his Philly Posse

Education: Senior at Maybell High School, shows little concern/effort there

Ethnicity: African-American

Religion: Baptist, son of a preacher

Dreams for the Future: None-he has a dismal outlook on life

Problems/Hardships: Coping with his mother's death

Clothing: Always baggy jeans and dark-colored pullovers or T-shirts (jokingly referred to as thug apparel)

Friends: The Philly Posse, Miles, Melvin, and Eric-like big brothers

Personality: Sensitive, although this is misleading; he plays everything off by bottling up his most passionate feelings and puts on a "tough guy" persona everywhere he goes

Positive Personal Habits: Focused, he is very good at planning

Undesirable Personal Habits: Possesses a stubborn streak and lies to himself

Home: Small ranch on a busy street in West Philadelphia

Fears: Bad dreams, the truth, being made fun of

Attitude: Pessimistic, dismal outlook on life

Dialect: Uses "Ebonics" or slang with his friends, known as a smooth talker

Complex: He changes drastically during the course of the story, becoming increasingly more understanding and open to the truth, letting stubbornness and indifference go by the wayside

Allegorical Connections: He represents what a man should be (by the end)

*All of these components help to make A.C. Dawson LIFELIKE

Writing Dialogue

Dialogue has to sound like speed, but it can't be a mere transcript; most people don't speak precisely or concisely enough to serve the writer's needs. According to Kilian, good dialogue has several functions:

♦ To convey exposition: to tell us, through the conversations of the characters, what we need to know to make sense of the story.

♦ To convey character: to show us what kinds of people we're dealing with.

♦ To convey a sense of place and time: to evoke the speech patterns, vocabulary and rhythms of specific kinds of people.

♦ To develop conflict: to show how some people use language to dominate others, or fail to do so.

Ask students to read their dialogue out loud; if it doesn't sound natural, or contains rhymes and rhythms, ask them to revise it.

Kilian suggests some hazards to avoid:

♦ Too much faithfulness to speech: "Um, uh, y'know, geez, well, like, well."

♦ Unusual spellings: "Yeah," not "Yeh" or "Yea" or "Ya."

♦ Too much use of "he said," "she said."

♦ Too much variation: "he averred," "she riposted."

- Dialect exaggeration: "Lawsy, Miz Scahlut, us's wuhkin' jes' as fas' as us kin."
- Excessive direct address: "Tell, me, Marshall, your opinion of Vanessa." "I hate her, Roger." "Why is that, Marshall?" "She bullies everyone, Roger."

See *Dialogue for "Mama's Boy"*.

Dialogue for "Mama's Boy"

"Adrian Christopher Dawson?" he asked anxiously, obviously baring back some anger.

"Yeah? My name's A.C. What do you want?" I retorted back, suddenly angry, too. I had a reason to be, didn't I? Nobody, and I mean nobody calls me Adrian 'cept Mama, and she gone. That's why I explode when people call me that name.

"A.C., then," he continued in vain.

"That's my name, don't wear it out!" I laughed. This was fun.

"You listen up right now, young man. I did not pick up this phone and dial your number to be disrespected. I'm calling to inform you that you're suspended for the rest of the week for your bad behavior."

"Wha'd I do this time, chief?" I asked smugly.

"You are such a trouble-maker. You're accused of vandalizing school property
for the third time this week."

"Oops! I'm so sorry, Mr. Schmidt. I didn't mean to do that. Honest! How can I ever make it up to you?"

Ask Students to Write the Short Story

The following is the story, "Mama's Boy," written by Patrick Alexander, Boardman High School. See *Assessment Rubric for a Short Story* on page 102.

"Mama's Boy"

Dear Journal:

It was a nightmare. The worst nightmare I've ever experienced. In fact, the worst part about this nightmare was that it was real. I shudder even now at the thought of its grave implications. This horrible, haunting image will never, ever go away. I remember it only in brief lapses of time. First, there was the cold, formidable nighttime sky, allowing only the full moon to add illumination to its dark countenance directly overhead. Then, from my seat in the kitchen where I'd been daydreaming, I heard a rush of footsteps, a heavy knock on our front door, and three quick rings on our doorbell. Before I could jump up from the dinner table to answer it, the front door flew open. Mama, her apron wrapped around her waist and rollers in her silky hair, calmly approached the entrance as I looked on in sheer disbelief. Our intruders, armed and motionless, stood before us in the doorway. There were two of them, their dark faces covered by ski masks. The bigger one sauntered in front of the other and shoved me against the wall.

"What you lookin' at, son? You 'fraid? Big as you is, ain't you gonna get the door fo' yo' mama?" he questioned.

Before I could choke out a response, he threw back his head, howling at the thought of a scornful reply of his own.

"Oh, forgive me, Shorty," he snarled between a series of snickers, "I done forgot already! You da mama's boy everyone 'round da 'hood be talking about, ain't you?"

I swallowed hard, but I don't remember responding to anything he said. In fact, I don't remember anything else happening until the second intruder suddenly came out of his stationary position at the doorway and held Mama at gunpoint. He kept repeating something in a high, squeaky voice, but I could not hear what he was saying. Seconds later, amid her helpless cries for mercy, he pulled the trigger, spraying her with a steady storm of bullets. The ear-splitting shots rang out until, hearing the whine of police sirens, he headed for the door. He paused momentarily, deciding what to say to me.

"Look here, you little mama's boy," he wailed, "if you say anything about this, I'll kill you too!" Content with these parting words, he darted out the door. The cops came and found me huddled over my mother, crying. The ambulance came and took her away from me. The neighbors came. My dad came. And I locked myself in my room, ashamed. Although later Dad told me otherwise, I had felt like Mama's killer. I had been responsible for my mother's death. I mean, I had stood there looking on as some weirdo shot her to death. What good had I been to her? I had let my own mother die, right before my very eyes.

I am a mama's boy, I had thought, crying myself to sleep.

Well, if you don't know it by now, I really hate bad dreams. I'm more afraid of them than anything else in the world. Ever since that night when Mama died (it's been a year now), I've had trouble sleeping. I swear... every night, a different part of her murder steals its way into my mind's eye... and then I wake up sobbing as I recall all the frightening details. I guess it's then when the "mama's boy" in me comes back. But I don't care. Nobody knows that I'm a mama's boy no more. Nobody knows, 'cept maybe me, my here journal, and my Lord. Wait a minute, I thought, pausing my writing. There I go again, lying to myself.

RING!!!

Great. There's the phone. You know, there's always something to interrupt a dude and his diary entries.

"Hey Dad, can you get the phone for me?" I hollered.

"Get it yourself!" he shouted back. "I'm in the middle of a really important transaction!"

Annoyed, I pushed my journal aside and picked up the phone. It was my high school principal, Mr. Schmidt.

"Adrian Christopher Dawson?" he asked anxiously, obviously baring back some anger.

"Yeah? My name's A.C. What do you want?" I retorted back, suddenly angry, too. I had a reason to be, didn't I? Nobody, and I mean nobody calls me Adrian 'cept Mama, and she gone. That's why I explode when people call me that name.

"A.C., then," he continued in vain.

"That's my name, don't wear it out!" I laughed. This was fun.

"You listen up right now, young man. I did not pick up this phone and dial your number to be disrespected. I'm calling to inform you that you're suspended for the rest of the week for your bad behavior. "

"Wha'd I do this time, chief?" I asked smugly.

"You are such a trouble-maker. You're accused of vandalizing school property for the third time this week."

"Oops! I'm so sorry, Mr. Schmidt. I didn't mean to do that. Honest! How can I ever make it up to you?"

I love being a jerk, I thought. It's so funny to see grown folks lose their cool over a few catchy phrases. And the best part about it is that I'm a natural at it.

"If you hate school so much, Mr. Dawson, I suggest you drop out like the rest of your good-for-nothing hoodlum cronies. I assure you: you'd be doing everyone here at Maybell High School a big favor. And another thing... Huh? Hello? Hello? "

See, I told you. I am a jerk. I hung up the phone right after Mr. Schmidt's last degrading comment. I guess it's 'cause I'm so sick and tired of being told who I am. I know who I am. I don't need nobody to put words in my mouth when it comes to who I am. I mean, I may be a jerk, maybe even a mama's boy. But there ain't no way that I'll ever be a high school dropout. I'm better than that. Graduation's a few months away, and it looks like I'll come out with a 3.4. Not bad for some kid who watched his mother get shot, huh? Not at all. Just as long as I do the stuff that'd make Mama proud, I certainly ain't doin' bad.

Suddenly, my thoughts were interrupted as I recalled my evening plans. I threw on my street clothes, a pair of some very old, very baggy black denim jeans, and a solid black hooded jacket, and ran downstairs. On the way down, I had to chuckle quietly to myself in remembering that Dad called these clothes "thug apparel." I slipped past him wordlessly, and left our quiet little ranch through the back door. Once outside, I inhaled deeply, taking in the horrible stench of gasoline. Now I know that's gotta sound funny. How could a neighborhood car repairman like myself hate the smell of gasoline? Thinking about it for a minute, I realized I couldn't answer that one. Looking ahead, I saw my Posse (that's what I call 'em, you know): Melvin, Miles, Eric, and Lance. Sickening as it may sound, these guys are the big brothers I never had.

"Yo A.C.! W'sup, man?" asked Lance, slapping hands with me.

"Nothin' much, man." I responded quickly. "Jus' da usual."

"Hey... what's got you down, A.C.?" Melvin asked, walking over. I had to force a smile at the sound of that all-too-familiar question. Melvin is always perfectly in tune with my emotions.

"Yo Pops ain't treatin' you right or somethin'?"

"Naw, naw man. Nothin' like dat. But there's somethin' I been thinkin' about."

They all huddled close together, partly because of the wintry air and partly because they wanted to hear what I had to say. I picked at my braids for a minute or two, deciding whether or not to spill the beans. Finally I spoke up.

"Y'all 'member how I... I used to act all sheepish and stuff?" I asked.

They nodded their heads, but it was as if saying those small words changed the whole world. Melvin shoved his hands into his pockets, Miles readjusted his stocking cap, and Eric looked up at a nearby streetlight. I hate it when we meet at street corners.

"What I'm gettin' at y'all," I said, slipping into my street language, "is dat... I still really miss my Mama. "

"Man don't be talkin' like dat! You know she dead and gone!" Eric snapped.

"Man, shut up!" I roared back. "You can't possibly know what it's like to lose somebody! You listen to me right now. I ain't no mama's boy. And I ain't just sayin' dat. I really ain't. Think about it: would a mama's boy go 'round town, vandalizing schools and houses like a door-to-door salesman? Huh? Would he be so rough and tough dat whenever anyone see him, dey walk the other direction, shakin' in dey boots? Huh?"

I cleared my throat for a minute, waiting for the power of my words to sink in. I glanced at my stolen Rolex, coughed, and continued, colder and harder than I had begun.

"And would a wimpy little mama's boy have da guts to go back to da man who killed his mama... and return da favor?"

That triggered about twenty reactions. Miles and Eric exchanged surprised glances.

"A.C.! What are you thinkin', man?" Miles demanded bluntly. He lined up with me, face-to-face, and stared directly into my eyes. I could feel his hot breath against my otherwise icy forehead. I noticed that his jeans were sagging incredibly low. They'd probably slide off at any minute now.

"You ain't gonna kill the dude who killed yo' mama, is you?" he inquired, concerned. "You don't even know who he is!"

"Look, I know his name is Shawn and he's been wanted for months!" I exclaimed. "And I also know dat as long as I live here in West Philly, ain't no policeman, no lawyer, o' no judge gonna extend justice fairly. So it's time fo' me to take matters into my own hands." I paused, thinking for something else to say. "My Mama ain't taught me much, but she taught me how to fight back when someone done wronged me."

"You have no idea what you're getting yourself into, man. Trust me. Or if you don't trust me, listen to yo' Pops. He a preacher, ain't he?"

I nodded quickly. My stubborn streak ordinarily wouldn't allow me to listen to religious advice, but I impatiently gave ear to what Miles had to say.

"God says somethin' like, 'Vengeance is mine,' if I do recall correctly. So uh… who are you to overstep His boundaries?"

I was becoming extremely flustered. I heard enough of this at home every night from my father West Philadelphia's pride and joy the Reverend Kenneth Dawson. His phony smile suddenly appeared in my mind. I truly detested Dad for forcing me to go to church with him every Sunday simply because he was, "The Pastor." All that so he could look good.

"Look, I appreciate your advice Miles," I said after a while, trying to be nice, "but I ain't got time for this 'What Would Jesus Do?' mess. Now, I found out dat our friend Shawn lives a block and a half from Lance's house, and I wanna put an end to his days of runnin' 'round like a blind fool. He ain't got no street smarts, so he'll be easy to track down. Now… is ya'll with me o' not?"

I presented my calloused hand in front of them, eagerly waiting for a response. A period of labored sighs followed. I was growing extremely impatient.

"Well?" I asked, letting out a sigh of my own. "What is ya'll doin'? You gonna stand 'round here, like a bunch o' mama's boys or what?"

That got to them. They joined hands with me, showing their intent to follow. Without waiting for any further comments, I whirled around, leading them through the busy, nighttime streets of West Philadelphia. As we trudged along wordlessly, I couldn't help but think how much of a big step this would be in my life. This would be the first time that "mama's boy" would prove himself as a true man, I thought, smiling bitterly. Mama would be proud. I glanced up. Oh no! Too late! I had bumped into a young woman carrying groceries. I apologized quickly. She smiled, forgiving me before I even got the muffled, "I'm sorry," out my mouth.

"What brings you out at this hour of night, anyways?" she asked.

Now, either I was extremely tired or she was extremely attractive or a combination of the two. Nevertheless, I blurted out my fiendish purpose without hesitation.

"I'm looking for a Shawn James of 1 Independence Avenue. Have you seen him?" She laughed heartily.

"No, silly!" she said, extending her hand in greeting. Yet I didn't register exactly what was going on. "I'm Shawn James," she continued. "Well, my full name is Shana Andrea James. It's a pleasure to meet you, young man."

I don't know exactly what I said or did at that precise moment, but I honestly felt like I could have died. Something was wrong. Something was very wrong.

"Well, don't just stand there!" she interjected. "Do something! Help a poor woman like me out, if nothing else!"

I stooped down to grab one of the bags when a nervous sensation swept over me. My temples pounding, sweat trickling down my thin sideburns, I let instinct take over. I had to be a man and not a mama's boy for once in my life. I had to get to the bottom of this. Even if Mama's killer was female, I had to even the score.

"I'm A.C. Dawson, the son of Anita Dawson," I started. "I'm sure you've heard of her… death. What I'm sayin' is… were you the one? Di-Did you… k-kill my Mama?"

"No!" she responded, almost hurt. She relaxed. "No, listen, dear, you've got it all wrong. I'm the detective assigned to find your mom's killer. I'm so sorry. I didn't know."

"It's okay!" I assured her gruffly. Tears were welling up in my eyes. I felt like a mama's boy all over again. I should be ashamed of myself, I thought, letting this get the best of me.

"Now look here," she said. "I've watched you, A.C. I've watched you a lot. You seem to have it all together. You're a tough guy, aren't you?"

I cleared my throat, and wiped my eyes quickly, trying to fit the "tough guy" image. "Yeah."

"But do you know what I think?" she asked. "I think that behind all those tattoos, the smooth talk, the thug mentality and your petty crimes … you're a really sweet, sensitive guy that knows who he is, but doesn't want to come out of his shell. Now am I on target?"

"Maybe," I responded bluntly.

"I don't know what it's like to lose someone," she continued. "But I do know what a man is. A man doesn't live in the past. A man doesn't let a loss get him down. A man doesn't hide from a helping hand. Yes, A.C., I know what a man is. And I think you're one of them." Finally letting her words sink in, I gave it all up. I embraced her gently, crying my eyes out. I ain't never cried like that. At least not since Mama died. I guess now I know why.

Assessment Rubric for a Short Story

	Exemplary	Excellent	Acceptable	Not Yet
Storyboard	8 to 10 cards with vivid scenes to envision and sequence the story	8 to 10 cards with excellent description of scenes to sequence the story	5 to 7 cards with enough information of the scenes to sequence the story	Information is too sketchy to envision much of a story; the scenes are ambiguous
Constructed Scene	Scene presents a complex problem for a character(s) and shows us how the characters deal with the problem; balances verbal and nonverbal content	The scene presents a problem and alludes to how the character deals with it; uses both verbal and nonverbal content	The scene presents a problem, but it is not clear how the character deals with it and may be lacking in verbal content or lacking in nonverbal description	The scene is too brief, lacking development of the character and the problem; still in the drafting stage
Character Resume	Character comes alive, believable, consistent; shows insight into the character's thoughts, beliefs, attitudes, personality, motivations	Excellent conceptualization of the character's thoughts, beliefs, attitudes, personality, motivations	The resume provides the basic information to begin visualizing the character; more details would help make the character more believable	Information is limited and inconsistent; underdeveloped; character not real and believable
Collage	Vivid images of the character's hobbies, interests, personality, family life, attitudes; artistic presentation	Excellent images to show the character's interests, personality, and family life. Excellent technical quality	Enough images to reveal some of the character's interests, personality and family life. Acceptable technical quality	Images are unorganized and inconsistent with the character resume; poor technical quality

Dialogue	Speech advances the story, revealing something new about the plot or the character; punctuated correctly; speech evokes the characters' personalities and motivations; characters speak naturally	Speech advances the story plot and the characters; punctuation is correct; speeches are concise; speech is used to convey character and develop conflict	Speech conveys the character, but the writer bogs down in chatter that doesn't advance the story; some errors in punctuation	Too many "he said," "she said," phrases; incorrect indentation and punctuation; speech does not reveal something new about the plot or character; too much direct address
Language/Style	Uses image, metaphor, and simile effectively; uses sentence variety; uses active voice; consistent style, tone, and point of view; grammatically correct; fluent prose; strong narrative voice; uses symbolism	Rich use of language to convey the story; uses active voice and sentence variety; mostly correct use of grammar; strong narrative voice	Limited use of language skills to convey the story; uses some passive voice; makes some errors in spelling and mechanics; narrative voice is emerging	Uses trite phrases, clichés, passive voice; limited use of language; incorrect sentences and misspellings; lack of sentence variety; voice is hidden or silenced
Introduction	Establishes the setting; sets the tone; introduces main character; establishes area of conflict; foreshadows the ending	Establishes the setting; introduces the main characters; the conflict or stress is not obvious; doesn't foreshadow the ending	Describes the setting and the main character; the stressful situation is missing; there is no foreshadowing	Description is too brief to visualize the setting and/or the main character. No allusion to the stress or conflict
Body	Tells story in scenes. Develops characters through action and dialogue; shows us what's going on; develops plot through increasingly serious problems; make solutions of problems appropriate to the characters	Tells the story in a series of scenes that contain a purpose, an obstacle or conflict, and a resolution; characters are developed mostly through dialogue; solutions are appropriate to the characters	Tells story in exposition; interesting plot and characters though not as fully developed as could be; some use of effective dialogue to carry the action; solution of problems is realistic; some repetition of details	Tells us, rather than shows us, the plot and characters; limited plot and character development; no use of dialogue; solutions not appropriate to the characters; repetition of details; telegraphed the punches
Conclusion	Presents a final, crucial conflict, a creative climax that reveals something to your readers that was not obvious or predictable	Presents an interesting, unexpected climax; surprise ending	Conclusion is somewhat predictable, but is appropriate for the story	Conclusion is too obvious, predictable, and unimaginative

Bibliography

Kilian, C. (April 2001). *Advice on novel writing* [Online]. Available: http://www.steampunk.com/sfch/writing/ckilian/.

9

UNDERSTANDING THE U.S. SOLDIER IN THE VIETNAM WAR: VIETNAM SCRAPBOOK

Joyce Rowland

Dedication from Richie's Mom in Fallen Angels

This scrapbook is for me. It is full of my thoughts and memories. This scrapbook is for my son Richie, who hasn't found the courage yet to remember all these memories I've saved. This scrapbook is also for anyone who has died in the war. May everyone who reads this find peace.

Katy Pemberton

Figure 9.1 Collage by Sarah Brown

Overview of Authentic Learning

The Vietnam War was unlike any other war the United States military has ever fought. The soldiers who fought, and especially those who returned, were not given the hero's welcome or the respect they so deserved. In order to understand and empathize with the plight of the soldier both in Vietnam and then back in the United States, students will put themselves in the place of Richard Perry (Fallen Angels by Walter Dean Myers) while reading of his ordeal as a soldier in the Vietnam War. Also, students will research terminology of the war before interviewing real men who fought in the war. This is especially important now, as many of today's students are the children and grandchildren of the generation of Vietnam veterans. Finally, a poignant way to learn about anyone would be by flipping through the pages of that person's own scrapbook, examining the pieces he or she cherished and kept safe for their sentimental value. Consequently, students will create a Vietnam Scrapbook based on a character related to Fallen Angels as a tool for exploring the gamut of emotions and trials experienced by the United States soldiers in Vietnam and by their families. Maybe a better understanding of the Vietnam veteran can help pull the generations together and build stronger family ties.

NCTE/IRA Standards

In this unit, students will:

◆ Keep a Reader's Response Log for Fallen Angels by Walter Dean Myers. In doing so, students will read a wide range of print to build an understanding of texts, of themselves, and of the cultures of the world (NCTE/IRA Standard #1); students will read a wide range of literature from many periods in many genres to build an understanding of the many dimensions of human experience (NCTE/IRA Standard #2); they will apply a wide range of strategies to comprehend, interpret, evaluate, and appreciate texts. They will draw on their prior experience, their interactions with other readers and writers, their knowledge of word meaning and of other texts, their word identification strategies, and their understanding of textual features (NCTE/IRA Standard #3); and students will use spoken, written, and visual language to accomplish their own purposes (NCTE/IRA Standard #12).

◆ Study Vietnam Vocabulary. In doing so, students will use a variety of technological and informational resources (e.g., libraries, databases, computer networks, video) to gather and synthesize information and to create and communicate knowledge (NCTE/IRA Standard #8).

◆ Create a Vietnam Family Scrapbook. In doing so, students will apply a wide range of strategies to comprehend, interpret, evaluate, and appreciate texts. They will draw on their prior experience, their interactions with other readers and writers, their knowledge of word meaning and of other texts, their word identification strategies, and their understanding of textual features (NCTE/IRA Standard #3); students will adjust their use of spoken, written, and visual language to communicate effectively with a variety of audiences and for different purposes (NCTE/IRA Standard #4); students will employ a wide range of strategies as they write and use various writing process elements appropriately to communicate with selected audiences for a variety of purposes (NCTE/IRA Standard #5); students will apply knowledge of language structure, language conventions (e.g., spelling and punctuation), media techniques, figurative language, and genre to create, critique, and discuss print and nonprint texts (NCTE/IRA Standard #6); students will develop an understanding of, and respect for, diversity in language use, patterns, and dialects across cultures, ethnic groups, geographic regions, and social roles (NCTE/IRA Standard #9); students will participate as knowledgeable, reflective, creative, and critical members of a variety of literacy communities (NCTE/IRA Standard #11); students will use spoken, written, and visual language to accomplish their own purposes (NCTE/IRA Standard #12).

Performance Tasks

Performance Task for Reader Response Logs for Richard Perry

Students are assigned the reading of the novel *Fallen Angels* by Walter Dean Myers. Students respond to what they are reading by keeping a Reader's Response Log to record their thoughts, associations, and opinions concerning the characters and events in each chapter of the novel. It is not a summary, but rather a personal discussion of what they think about the events that are happening in the novel. They should especially be looking to trace the moral and spiritual development of the main character, Richard Perry. Then, after each five or six chapters (to be determined by the teacher), special projects and small discussion groups will be required to supplement students' individual responses. See *Assessment Rubric for Reader Response Logs* on page 110 based on categories of response suggested by Hancock (2000).

- After the first five chapters, ask students to write the letter that Richard Perry wrote home to his mom telling about Jenkins' death (which he later tore up). Students could model their letters according to the ones in *Dear America: Letters Home from Vietnam* edited by Bernard Edelman (1985), but must remain true to Richie's experiences and perspective.

- After Chapter 11, within the response discussion groups, assign each group to focus on one of the following four topics:

- the newsmen filming the killing of the one Viet Cong (as if he were a trophy)
- the fight between Wallowick and Johnson
- Richard Perry on patrol with the group that shot the other American patrol
- the death of Lt. Carroll

♦ Near the end of the book, have students make a character continuum similar to the one suggested by Milner and Milner (1999). This activity clarifies the relationships of characters, one to another, by locating them on different continua. Provide long sheets of paper, as from a roll of paper (about 4 to 5 feet long). In small groups, the students decide the two ends of their spectrum, such as most brave to least brave, or most caring to least caring. Then, using magazine pictures or drawing their own pictures, they choose symbols for each character in the book and place them on their continuum. Students should be given opportunity to "show and tell" their continuum to the rest of the class.

♦ Following the reading of the final chapters, students will write a letter to the school board justifying the value of reading this book in high school. See *Student Excerpts from Letters to the School Board.*

Student Excerpts from Letters to the School Board

Dear Members of the School Board:

As a junior, I have read the book Fallen Angels. I learned a lot from this book and would recommend any class to study this as we have. As a student, I never quite understood how bad it was for the soldiers in the Vietnam War. I always thought it was older people who served. However, I now know that is not at all true. This book made me start to think and feel like I was a soldier in the middle of the war...

Most kids my age don't like to read. I am one of them. I don't have the time. However, once you start into it, you can't put it down. You make time to read it. It's not only exciting, but it also makes you think. If you don't let kids read Fallen Angels and study about the Vietnam War, you are taking away the privilege of learning about a big part of our history.
Leigh Ann Imhoff

The story of Fallen Angels really touched me. At first the language caught me off guard, but by the end of the story, I didn't even notice it. When I was done, it also made sense how the words and atmosphere were *relevant. This book is more than appropriate for students in the years to come. I never really thought of Vietnam before we did this section in English. After reading the book, everything about Nam became real to me. I think this book is vital to students to be reading.*

Heather A. Hood

In spite of the language, this book has a lot of heart. It makes you think about life and your own self worth. The language in this book needs to be there because it goes with the times of the war. It helps you feel the extremities of the war.

Nathan Fincham

This is the only book, in my entire school career, that I have actually enjoyed reading, and it's kept my attention.

Cindy Hawkins

Performance Task for Learning Vietnam Vocabulary

Instruct students to find the definitions for the vocabulary words provided in the Word List below from the novel *Fallen Angels*. To find the definitions, they should go to http://www.altavista.com and search for "Glossary of Military Terms & Slang from the Vietnam War." If the Web site listing only shows letters A-C, they should click on "show other pages from this site," and it will show three other sites to cover the rest of the alphabet. Students should write the definition down on the word list. Then ask students to choose three of the terms and explain in a short paragraph what importance that term had in the book. See *Grading Criteria for Vietnam Vocabulary* on page 111.

Word List

Cong (1), hooch (19), in country (17), RPG (22), flak jacket (26), in the deep (28), the boonies (28), dog tags (42), body bags (43), angel warriors (44), Willy Peters (49), Chie Hoi (50), ARVN (51), gooks (54), latrine (61), LZ (63), fox hole (71), trip flares (70), Hueys (78), clip (80), bandoliers (98), rucksack (100), OCS (101), medevacs (104), Pacification Mission (108), DMZ, The World (309), claymore mines (122), spider hole (202), HQ (170), NVA (153), M-16 (33), M-60 (33).

Assessment Rubric for Reader Response Logs

	Self-Directed Responder	*Mature Responder*	*Emerging Responder*	*Novice Responder*
Independent Reader Responses	Evidence of deep involvement and personal interactions with characters and events of the story; incorporates powerful writing to share opinions, emotions and thoughts; rich discussion indicating extended thought	Willing to use writing to share personal opinions, emotions, and thoughts about the novel; evidence of involvement with the main characters by conversing with them; responses are similar to what others might share	Shares reactions through writing, but the entries maintain a detached commitment or connection to the text; the response conveys duty rather than genuine interest	Writes a number of brief responses that merely fulfill an assignment, rather than sharing a commitment to the text and characters; entries seem hasty, many are brief, sketchy
Letter Home	Letter is consistent with Richie's character development; makes reference to events in the text; conveys a personal message to his family	Letter is consistent with Richie's character development, but doesn't make reference to the text; conveys a likely message to his family	Letter is not consistent with Richie's character development and departs from the text; conveys a stereotypical message to his family	Letter shows a lack of understanding of Richie's character development and little understanding of his situation; letter is brief
Discussion Group Report	Evidence of multiple perspectives; accurate information; elaborate details about the people and events; quotes from the text	Strong opinion, detailed in the description of the people or events; accurate information; adequate details; some textual evidence	Detached insights into the characters and events, maintaining a distance from deeper involvement with the story	Summarizes or retells the story rather than interacting with the text; some comprehension is evident, but the response is sketchy
Character Continuum	Character traits are unique to major themes of the novel; creative symbols to represent characters; insight into placement of characters on the continuum	Creative character traits for the continuum; appropriate symbols to represent characters; excellent rationale for placement of characters on continuum	Character traits are stereotypical; acceptable symbols to portray characters; questionable placement of characters on the continuum	Character traits are not the antithesis; symbols are questionable; placement of characters on the continuum is questionable
Persuasive Letter to Board of Education	Opens with a hook and provides convincing and personal arguments of the redeeming values for reading the novel	Creates a favorable impression, but not a hook in the opening; convincing arguments showing personal values, but could appeal to more universal ones	Grabs reader's attention, but appeals to stereotypical arguments; needs more specifics and details	Does not grab the reader's attention; discussion is not convincing to make a change; lacks supporting details; needs editing to fix mechanical errors

---
Grading Criteria for Vietnam Vocabulary
---

5 = Fully Achieved; 3 = Partially Achieved, 0 = Not Achieved   Score (20)

Your work will be graded according to the extent to which your responses incorporate the following criteria:

- Includes a clear, accurate, complete definition for all 32 terms on the _____ word list

- Includes a paragraph for one of the terms explaining the impor- _____ tance of the term in the novel.

- Includes a paragraph for a second term explaining the importance _____ of the term in the novel.

- Includes a paragraph for a third term explaining the importance of _____ the term in the novel.

Performance Task for Vietnam War Terms

- ◆ Provide time in class for each student to write a reflection paper on what they already know about the Vietnam War. Share in small groups, and then have each group give a short oral summary of their discussion.

- ◆ Assign each student one to three terms related to the Vietnam War or the cultural responses to the Vietnam War. Below is a suggested list:
  - Jane Fonda and the Anti-War Movement
  - The North Vietnamese Army
  - Conscientious Objectors
  - The Paris Peace Talks/Agreement
  - The Ho Chi Minh trail
  - The Gulf of Tonkin Incident and Resolution
  - French Colonialism in Vietnam
  - The Early Years: 1955–1964
  - LBJ Goes to War: 1964–1968
  - Posttraumatic Stress Disorder
  - The Kent State Shootings
  - Anti-War and Protest Songs
  - The Army of the Republic of Vietnam (South Vietnam)
  - Agent Orange and its effect on soldiers and on the land
  - Battle of Hue
  - The Draft

- The Fall of Saigon
- The My Lai Massacre
- The Viet Cong (tunnel tactics)
- The Invasion of Cambodia
- The Siege of Khe Sahn
- Geography of Vietnam
- POWS/MIAS
- The Vietnam Memorial
- The Weapon of the War
- Daniel Ellsberg and the Pentagon Papers
- Vietnamese Refugees-Boat People
- Women who Served in Vietnam
- Ho Chi Minh (the person)
- The Battle of Dienbienphu

♦ Assign the students to research their term(s) on the Internet, beginning by going to http://www.altavista.com and searching Vietnam War terms, which should give them a very good listing of appropriate sites to use.

♦ Students must prepare to explain/tell the definition of their term and its importance to the war. To accomplish this, they must research several sites and choose the best one to show to the class via the LCD projector during their explanation. Also, they may show other research materials that apply, such as books, photographs, magazine or newspaper articles, video clips, etc.

♦ Students will present their findings to the class in a five-minute explanation/presentation. Other students in the class must take notes on the presentations. At first, it may seem awkward because the students do not know much about the time period, but as more students present, the big picture will become clearer. Time should be allotted between presentations for some discussion. See *Grading Criteria for Vietnam War Terms*.

Grading Criteria for Vietnam War Terms

---

5 = Fully Achieved; 3 = Partially Achieved; 0 = Not Achieved   Score (15)

Your work will be graded according to the extent to which your responses incorporate the following criteria:

- Creative and informative presentation   _____

- Insight into the important connections to the war   _____

- Effective visual representation of the term   _____

Performance Task for Interviewing a Vietnam Veteran

♦ Instruct students to log onto the Internet and to go to the URL http://www.spartacus.schoolnet.co.uk/vietinterview.htm. This is a Web site that enables students to interview veterans by e-mailing them. On the Web site, they will find biographical sketches of six to eight people who served in Vietnam in some capacity. These biographies reflect a variety of values concerning the war. Students should read all the biographies and then choose one person for whom they will prepare an interview.

♦ Students will be given instruction on creating interview questions that elicit a worthwhile response. Students should prepare a set of interview questions (minimum of seven, maximum of ten questions). Students will exchange and peer edit the list of questions.

♦ Students will go back to the Web site and submit the interview. When the students receive their responses, they will first write a reflection paper in which they discuss what they learned from the interview, and then they will use the information gathered to write entries in the scrapbook they will create from the viewpoint of one of the characters in the book. (This scrapbook is their final project for the unit.) See *Grading Criteria for Interview of a Vietnam Veteran.*

Grading Criteria for an Interview of a Vietnam Veteran

---

5 = Fully Achieved; 3 = Partially Achieved; 0 = Not Achieved   Score (20)

Your work will be graded according to the extent to which your responses incorporate the following criteria:

• Questions elicited thoughtful responses   _____

• Questions elicited various perspectives   _____

• Reflection paper showed a compassionate position   _____

• Responses were mechanically correct   _____

Performance Task for Vietnam War Issue Survey

♦ With a partner, students will create a hypothesis about an issue concerning the Vietnam War or the cultural response to the Vietnam War or Vietnam War veterans today. Next they will create five questions that will prove or disprove the hypothesis.

♦ Students will survey a random sampling of the student body using the five survey questions. At least 25 percent of the student body must be surveyed.

- ◆ Students will chart the results on a table and on some type of graph on the computer (line graph, bar graph, histograph, pie graph).

- ◆ Collaboratively, students will draw their conclusions and write up the results with their conclusions. They should attach their report to the graph for display purposes.

- ◆ Individually, students will respond to what they learned by doing this survey (minimum 150 words). See *Teacher-Generated Sample of Vietnam Issue Hypothesis and Survey Questions. See Grading Criteria for Vietnam War Issue Survey.*

Teacher-Generated Sample of Vietnam Issue Hypothesis and Survey Questions

Hypothesis: The Vietnam War is not being adequately taught in schools today.

Survey Questions:

- ◆ Did you ever hear of the Vietnam War?

- ◆ What countries fought in the Vietnam War?

- ◆ Have you ever been given opportunity to read about and discuss the Vietnam War in a history class?

- ◆ Who won the war?

Would what happened in the Vietnam War influence whether you would sign up with a branch of the military to fight for your country if we went to war today?

Grading Criteria for Vietnam War Issue Survey

5 = Fully Achieved; 3 = Partially Achieved; 0 = Not Achieved   Score (30)

Your work will be graded according to the extent to which your responses incorporate the following criteria:

- • Creative hypothesis concerning the Vietnam War   _____

- • Five questions that will prove or disprove the hypothesis   _____

- • Evidence of random sampling of student body   _____

- • Table or graph of results   _____

- • Report of conclusions   _____

- • Individual self-reflection paper   _____

Performance Tasks for Vietnam Scrapbook Project

Here is a chance to let your creative juices flow!

♦ You will be assigned a character either from the book Fallen Angels, or a fictitious relative of one of the characters in the book. Your job is to create a scrapbook from your character's point of view.

♦ Make it evident that you have read Fallen Angels and that you understand the feelings of the time period through the eyes of your character.

♦ This must be historically accurate, emotionally moving, and artistically appealing. This is our last big project. Show what you have learned! Create a picture of what experiencing the Vietnam War was really like. Take time with this. Substandard work is not acceptable. Go all out!

♦ The scrapbook must include at least the following list. Extraordinary effort will be rewarded. See *Assessment Rubric for Vietnam Scrapbook* on page 120.

  • A cover that would have been created by your character.

  • At least two created, but accurate, news articles with headlines detailing historical events important to your character.

  • At least five pictures or photos (real or created) that depict family or group events relevant to your character.

♦ Any medals of honor earned by your veteran, including the certificate or paperwork that would accompany it, or any warning letters for desertion.

♦ Death notices, or letters.

♦ At least three letters written to or from family or friends. (See on page 116 *Excerpts from Letters for Scrapbook for Brew*, by Nathan Fincham, whose scrapbook was in the character of Brew.)

  • One letter to your state congressional representative concerning a true event, written from your character's perspective, of course. This must be typed and written in formal language. (See *Letter to a Congressman* on page 117, written by Sarah Brown.)

  • The response letter from the congressional person, typed on letterhead. (See *Response Letter from the Congressman* on page 118, written by Sarah Brown.)

  • The lyrics to one song that affected your character, with comments explaining why the song had this effect.

  • The words to one poem that affected your character, with comments explaining why the poem had this effect.

- Three diary entries concerning a war or domestic event. (See *Journal Entry Portraying the Character of Richie's Mom* on page 119, by Katy Pemberton.)
♦ Assign or have students pick a card that has on it one of the following characters' name (note that some of the characters are from the book and some have been fabricated):
  - Family # 1 = Perry, Kenny, Mom
  - Family #2 = Lobel, Dad
  - Family #3 = PeeWee, Earlene (ex-girlfriend), Sister (engaged to helicopter pilot in Vietnam)
  - Family #4 = Brew, Mom (homemaker), Dad (Methodist minister), Brother (20-year-old conscientious objector)
  - Family #5 = Judy Duncan, Mom (worker in a factory), Dad (worker in a factory), Sister (19-year-old college student-involved in anti-war protests)

You may converse with your "selected family" to gather ideas, but all the work in the scrapbook for your character must be your own.

Excerpts from Letters for Scrapbook for Brew

Dear Mom,

. . . How can God just stand by and watch so much blood shed? Why can people hate so much? Why bring me into it? I had nothing to do with starting this war but I'm over here fighting it. It doesn't make sense. Why should I risk my life for people I don't know to kill people I don't hate? It just isn't right! What I want to do is stay home with my family. . . .

Love,
Brew

Dear Son,

. . . The Peace Talks are going good. If things go well, you'll be home soon. Just hold out a little longer. God's going to bring you home.

This war should never have been started. How can so much hate exist? But earth is a taste of Hell. And forcing young men to fight for a country that doesn't even respect their sacrifice. . . it just sickens me.

Love,
Mom

To Mr. and Mrs. Brewster:

My name is Perry and I knew your son....I'm sorry but your son didn't make it....I know Brew had plans to be a preacher. I think he would have served God well, but I guess it just wasn't in God's plan. I don't know why God took him and not me.

None of this can possibly help make you feel any better. I wish I could take all your pain from you, but I can't. Just remember, Brew died still loving and serving God...

Sincerely,
Richie Perry

Letter to a Congressman

1654 West Highland St.
Monrovia, CA 56987

Mr. Bob Walters
United States Congress
1564 N. Liberty Street
Washington, D.C. 45629

Dear Sir:

My name is Lobel and I have just finished serving a year with the United States Army in Vietnam. I enlisted as soon as I heard of the need for soldiers for the Vietnam War. I was glad and willing to be able to serve my country. I cannot believe that there was a need for a draft, and that young men would not think it an honor to serve their country. One matter of the draft, though, that really upsets me is the fact that college students are exempt.

Exempting college students is being very unfair, as not all students have that same opportunity to be able to attend a college and keep them from the hells of war. Exempting college students helps the rich while it hurts the poor, underprivileged people. Some people do not have an opportunity to go to college without first going to the army and taking advantage of its scholarship opportunities. The majority of college students are wealthy, upper-class white folks, leaving the draftees to be all the poor whites and blacks and other minorities, who already have enough of a disadvantage without having to fight a war. This discrimination needs to stop; the draft should not play favorites but rather should treat everyone as equals. We should all be proud to serve our great nation in her time of need.

I hope you take into serious consideration what I have mentioned and work to see that college students are no longer exempt from the draft and that everyone has fair and equal rights when it comes to being drafted. Thank you for your time.

Sincerely,
Adam C. Lobel

Response Letter from the Congressman

United States Congress
1564 Liberty St.
Washington, D.C. 45629

Adam C. Lobel
1654 West Highland St.
Monrovia, CA 56987

Dear Mr. Lobel:

I would like to commend you for volunteering to help your country and also for being proud of it. It is a great honor to be able to help your country in her time of need. We need more intelligent, patriotic citizens like you. It pains me that I was not able to enter into battle myself, but I have been working hard to aid our country's cause.

I would like to thank you for taking the time to write to me, showing your concern about the matter of college students being exempted from the draft. I have received many letters, many from Vietnam veterans like yourself, concerning this issue. Many people believe as strongly as you do that it is a very unfair, biased law. I hold the same belief as you do, and I do not see why one person should be exempted simply due to the fact that they are getting further education. I believe the only reason to be excused from an honorable duty that your country is asking you to do would be on account of a physical handicap of some sort. I, myself, came from a poor family and I know what hard work is like and how unfair life can be sometimes. I assure you that I will work hard and press for unbiased laws that are fair to all of America's proud citizens.

Sincerely,
Bob Walters

Journal Entry Portraying the Character of Richie's Mom

Dear Journal,

Oh my God, oh my God! He's wounded. My baby is thousands of miles away and he is hurt. What do I do? I want to cry, but I can't. I just want to get there as fast as I can and hold his hand, but I can't.

Is he alone? Is he scared? I don't know and Mama should always know about her babies....

They came to tell me. Soldiers in uniforms came with a telegram. My heart stopped, fell, and wrenched in my chest, all at the same time. I'd never gotten a telegram before. They handed it to me, tipped their hats, and said, "The army's condolences to you, Ma'am," whatever that means. I read the telegram and all those stops confused me. I read it again and I knew and I understood. You were hurt. How, where, and why I didn't know.

Could I believe the government? How did I know you weren't really dead. I can't erase the terrible things in my mind.

Even now the red ink of this pen makes me sick to my stomach. I have come to a decision. Something I've avoided, but something I have to do. Something I should have done a long time ago. I'm going to stop drinking. I want to be the best Mama I can be.... Richie is going to need me when he gets home.

Assessment Rubric for Vietnam Scrapbook

Components	Exceptional 5 Points	Acceptable 4 Points	Not Yet 0–3 Points
Cover	Critical information provided; artistic	Critical information provided; no graphics	Critical information missing; no graphics
News Article	The piece has a clear focus, connects to the topic well, with clearly developed thoughts and details; highly significant message	The piece is relevant to the topic, but lacks clarity and information; message is less significant	The piece is ambiguous in connection to the topic and lacks a sustained focus. Message is unclear
Pictures/ Photos (5)	High quality, appropriate, meaningful, expressive, relevant to your character	Appropriate, realistic for your character, not as high quality	Inappropriate for the character; not all 5 are present
Medals of Honor or Warning Letter for Desertion	Celebrates the victories of your veteran or reprimands and warns about desertion	Adequate description of the honors or convincing warning about desertion.	Inadequate description of the honors or inadequate warning letter
Death Notice/ Letter	Respectful letter to the family explaining the circumstance of the death	Acceptable letter to the family explaining the circumstance of the death	Inadequate letter due to lack of details and mechanical errors
Letter Written to Family or Friends	The letter details an event that happened to the character; is personal and friendly; considers the audience	The letter describes an event that occurred to the character, but is less personal and/or less detailed and less aware of the audience	The letter mentions an event in the book to the character, is impersonal, and may be inappropriate for the character; too many errors
Letter Written from Family or Friends	The letter details an event that happened to the character; is personal and friendly; considers the audience	The letter describes an event that occurred to the character, but is less personal and/or less detailed and less aware of the audience	The letter mentions an event in the book to the characte, is impersonal, and maybe inappropriate for the character; too many errors
Response Letter to Family or Friends	The letter details an event that happened to the character; is personal and friendly; considers the audience	The letter describes an event that occurred to the character, but is less personal and/or less detailed and less aware of the audience; some errors	The letter mentions an event in the book to the character, is impersonal, and maybe inappropriate for the character; many errors
Letter to Congressman	Relates a true event, represents an issue or concern of your character, uses formal English, typed on letterhead; gives a compelling and well-supported plea; correct	Relates a true event, represents your character's concerns, uses mostly formal English, typed on letterhead; argument is somewhat stereotypical	Does not relate a true event; does not represent your character's perspective, may not be typed and may have errors; argument is vague or sketchy
Letter from Congressman	The letter acknowledges your request and takes a strong position either for or against it; typed on letterhead	The letter addresses your issue and takes a position for or against it; typed on letterhead	The letter fails to address your concerns and doesn't have a realistic response; may not be typed

Lyrics to One Song with Comments	The lyrics clearly express the emotions and concerns of your character; excellent associations and connections to the character	The lyrics express the concerns of the character; good explanation and connections made for your choice	The lyrics are loosely connected to the character's situation; the connections to the character are vague
Words of One Poem with Comments	The poem creatively expresses a main point or image that affected your character; uses rich poetic language; includes an explanation	The poem expresses a point or image that affected the character, but is not as focused or doesn't use many poetic elements; the explanation is sketchy	The poem fails to express the perspective of the character and does not use poetic language; the explanation is missing
Diary Entry Concerning a War Event	Entry includes detailed, even moving, reflection of the thoughts, feelings, and associations made of the character concerning a war event	Entry includes an adequate reflection on the experience or event and is personal, though not moving	The entry is sketchy and ambiguous, demonstrating limited control of language and thought
Diary Entry Concerning a Domestic Event	Entry includes detailed, even moving, reflection of the thoughts, feelings, and associations made of the characte concerning a war event	Entry includes an adequate reflection on the experience or event and is personal, though not moving	The entry is sketchy and ambiguous, demonstrating limited control of language and thought
Diary Entry of Your Choice	Entry includes detailed, even moving, reflection of the thoughts, feelings, and associations made of the character concerning a war event	Entry includes an adequate reflection on the experience or event and is personal, though not moving	The entry is sketchy and ambiguous, demonstrating limited control of language and thought
Overall Artistic Appeal	The project is neat, complete, reflects the character's personality, well-organized, attractive, colorful, high-quality	The project is neat, complete, and approximates the character's personality; the artistic appeal is not noteworthy	The project is not neat, complete, or well-organized; it does not reflect the character's personality; no artistic appeal
Overall Emotional Appeal	Moving, compelling, maybe sentimental, use of language. Strong personal commitment to the character	Some emotional commitment, but not unusual or compelling	Very objective and detached
Overall Historical Accuracy	Reflects accurate research and understanding of the Vietnam War era	Mostly correct portrayal of the Vietnam War era, but needs more direct references to real events	Inaccurate portrayal of the Vietnam War era through your character's eyes
Overall Creative Presentation	Creative approach to the project; great imagination and ability to role play your character	Acceptable approach to the project, though not highly imaginative	Lacking imagination, organizational skills; limited use of language
Total (100)			

Bibliography

Edelman, B. (1985). *Dear America: Letters home from Vietnam.* New York: Pocket Books, Simon & Schuster.

Hancock, M. (2000). *A celebration of literature and response: Children, books, and teachers in K-8 classrooms.* Columbus, OH: Merrill, Prentice Hall.

Milner, J. O., & Milner, L. F. M. (1999). *Bridging English,* (2nd ed.). Upper Saddle River, NJ: Prentice Hall.

Myers, W. D. (1988). *Fallen angels.* New York: Scholastic.

10

ARCHAEOLOGICAL LITERACY DIG

Janie Reinart

I became aware that writing was based on words, that they came out of my mind, and that I had to trust what I thought, felt, and saw. I could not be afraid that I was insignificant, or stupid—or, I could be afraid, but I had to speak anyway.

Natalie Goldberg

Overview of Authentic Learning

How do students realize that they are writers and give voice to their writing as an essential part of their lives? Students dig up writing from their past as well as find present-day artifacts to create a display board for this project. This entire literacy history is merged together by a metaphor that relates to the student's life. The activity also builds community spirit as students learn more about themselves and each other. A teacher-generated rubric assesses outcome. Upon completion, students will display projects. Class time is used to visit each site as students use signed Post-it notes to make positive comments about individual display boards. Modeling is important! Teachers are encouraged to create a display board to share with the class. Using this project at the start of a class is effective and helps to build a writing community as students get to know each other. This project could be assigned the first day of class, but students will need at least one weekend for preparing the display board.

NCTE/IRA Standards

In this assessment, students will:

- Create a literacy history of their development as a writer by providing artifacts for a display board. In doing so, they will use spoken, written, and visual language to accomplish their own purposes (NCTE/IRA Standard #12) and will participate as knowledgeable, reflective, creative, and critical members of a variety of literacy communities (NCTE/IRA Stand #11).

- Create a metaphor that serves as a theme for their project. In doing so, students will adjust their use of spoken, written, and visual language to communicate effectively with a variety of audiences and for different purposes (NCTE/IRA Standard #4); they will employ a wide range of strategies as they write and use different writing process elements appropriately to communicate with different audiences for a variety of purposes (NCTE/IRA Standard #5); and they will apply knowledge of language structure, language conventions, media techniques, figurative language, and genre to create, critique, and discuss print and nonprint texts (NCTE/IRA Standard #6).

- Critique classmate's display boards as well as complete a self-evaluation. In doing so, students will develop an understanding of and respect for diversity in language use, patterns, and dialects across cultures, ethnic groups, geographic regions, and social roles (NCTE/IRA Standard #9) and they will employ a wide range of strategies as they write and use different writing process elements appropriately to communicate with different audiences for a variety of purposes (NCTE/IRA Standard #5).

Materials

- Post-it notes
- Display board
- Directions/Rubric
- Metaphor worksheet
- Sample Archeological Literacy Dig (could be teacher constructed)

Performance Tasks

- Ask the question: "How many of you think of yourself as writers?" Teachers take a survey of the class by using a show of hands. Explain that students are going to discover how they have developed as writers over the years. Show an example of an archeological dig, if one is available, or one of your own writing pieces.

- Ask students to collect artifacts of their writing from as far back as they can find. These could be drawings, letters, diaries, cards, paintings, early writings, report cards, recital programs, thank-you notes, poetry, and short stories. They will need to ask their parents, family, and friends to help them recreate the history of their literacy.

♦ After students have collected their artifacts, ask them to create a metaphor that would make a statement about their works. Hand out the metaphor worksheet with the due date of the project (See *Archaeological Literacy Dig Metaphor Worksheet* on page 126).

♦ On the day that students turn in display boards, use the entire period (and more time if needed) for students to comment with Post-it notes and admire classmate's work (See *Assessment Rubric for Archaeological Literacy Dig* on page 127). Suggestion: This is a great project to use for Open House (store folded display boards in a corner of the room until needed). Have parents write comments to their children using Post-it notes.

♦ Self-Evaluation—After students write comments to each other about their projects, have them write a reflection on what they saw and felt. Share reflections in class. Take the survey again. Students will look at writing from a different perspective.

Wayne Mittwede's Archeological Dig

Archaeological Literacy Dig Metaphor Worksheet

Dig back into your past and discover how you became a writer. Uncover artifacts that show the roots of your writing (drawings, letters, diaries, cards, etc.). Ask your parents, family, and friends for help in finding relics of your writing from early drawings to present day keep sakes. Build a bridge to the present by including objects that exhibit how you use writing now in your everyday life. Connect the examples on your display board with a theme that is unique to your life by using a metaphor. A metaphor is a figure of speech that makes a comparison between dissimilar things.

Here is an example:

Words weave their way through the fabric of my life piecing things together into a quilt of experiences.

♦ Select one noun (e.g., words, letters, writing).

♦ Select a theme (unique to your life) and two related concrete nouns (I chose fabric, quilt or basketball game, contest).

♦ Pick a verb and a participle (I chose weave, piecing or dribble, scoring).

♦ Pick another noun (things or points).

♦ Pick a prepositional phrase (into a quilt of experiences or in the contest of experience)

♦ Create your metaphor:

Writing dribbles its way through the basketball game of my life scoring points in the contest of experience.

Brainstorm ideas:

Assessment Rubric for Archeological Literacy Dig

	Exemplary	*Acceptable*	*Incomplete*
Design	Creative use of color, pictures, graphics and text. Size and layering is purposeful and adds to the overall quality of the display	The display captures the viewer's attention, but has limited use of color, pictures, graphics and text	The display is not well developed and lacks visual appeal and organization
Artifacts (Writing Pieces)	Project includes a large number of writing pieces and a variety of genres showing the range of development and interests of the writer	Project includes an acceptable number of writing pieces, but limited genres. There are pieces showing development over time	Project includes a limited number of writing pieces and genres. The pieces do not show a development over time
Concept (Theme, Metaphor)	Metaphor excels in communicating the personality and development of the writer	Metaphor reflects the development of the writer's interests.	The theme is not stated as a metaphor
Self-Evaluation	Reflects on strengths and problems of the experience; sets goals for future writing; comments on classmates' projects	Main focus of the reflective experience is based on summarizing the artifacts; doesn't indicate future goals or insights	Descriptive as opposed to reflective. Limited to "I liked or disliked this project because…"

Bibliography

Goldberg, N. (1990). *Wild mind.* New York: Bantam Books.

11

WOMEN IN THE WORKFORCE: A PROJECT USING THE FUTURE PROBLEM-SOLVING MODEL

Ruth McClain

Act quickly, think slowly.

Greek Proverb

Overview of Authentic Learning

Sophocles' *Antigone* provides a backdrop for students to think about the conflicts between men and women in the world today. Antigone is caught between obedience to her king and family honor. Should she submit to the king's authority to leave her brother without proper burial or should she bury him under penalty of death? After students discuss Antigone's decisions and solutions to her moral dilemma, they will consider modern situations. A Young Adult novel that could be paired with this play is Make Lemonade by Virginia Euwer Wolff. In this novel, a single teenage mother with two children struggles to make ends meet on minimum wage, confronts harassment, and finally goes back to school. The video *Norma Rae*, played by Sally Field, is the tale of a naïve textile worker, widow, and mother in the South who becomes empowered by standing up for her rights in the workplace. Regardless of the materials used to teach this assessment, students will create a project log requiring them to solve moral dilemmas that women encounter in the workplace today using the six-step model of the Future Problem Solving Program, Inc. (FPSP), International Office, 202B Regency Road, Lexington, KY 40503.

NCTE/IRA Standards

For this Project Log Assessment, students will:

♦ Read the play, Antigone, by Sophocles, and write project log entries about gender-related issues raised in the play. In doing so, students will apply a wide range of strategies to comprehend, interpret, evaluate, and appreciate texts. They will draw on their prior experience, their interactions with other readers and writers, their knowledge of word meaning and of other texts, their word identification strategies, and their understanding of textual features (NCTE/IRA Standard #3).

♦ Identify a gender issue in the work place and research background information on the topic. In doing so, students will conduct research on issues and interests by generating ideas and questions, and by posing problems. They will gather, evaluate, and synthesize data from a variety of sources to communicate their discoveries in ways that suit their purpose and audience (NCTE/IRA Standard #7); and, they will develop an understanding of, and respect for, diversity in language use, patterns, and dialects across cultures, ethnic groups, geographic regions, and social roles (NCTE/IRA Standard #9).

♦ Process their research in order to identify possible problems and their potential solutions. In doing so, students will conduct research on issues and interests by generating ideas and questions, and by posing problems. They will gather, evaluate, and synthesize data from a variety of sources to communicate their discoveries in ways that suit their purpose and audience (NCTE/IRA Standard #7); and, they will participate as knowledgeable, reflective, creative, and critical members of a variety of literacy communities (NCTE/IRA Standard #11).

♦ Analyze a workplace scenario based on the topic using the Future Problem Solving six-step model. In doing so, students will participate as knowledgeable, reflective, creative, and critical members of a variety of literacy communities (NCTE/IRA Standard #11) and they will use spoken, written, and visual language to accomplish their own purposes (NCTE/IRA Standard #12).

♦ Write a paper about significant issues using a variety of writing modes. In doing so, students will use spoken, written, and visual language to accomplish their own purposes (NCTE/IRA Standard #12); they will adjust their use of spoken, written, and visual language to communicate effectively with a variety of audiences and for different purposes (NCTE/IRA Standard #4); they will employ a wide range of strategies as they write and use different writing process elements appropriately to communicate with different audiences for a variety of purposes (NCTE/IRA Stand #5); and they will apply knowledge of language structure, language conventions, media techniques, figurative language, and genre to create, critique, and discuss print and nonprint texts (NCTE/IRA Standard #6).

Performance Tasks for the Project Log

Questions Based on *Antigone*

♦ Ask students to read Sophocles' *Antigone* and write project log entries for the following questions (taken from the Classics Technology Center: http://ablemedia.com/ctcweg/netshots/):

• After they have read the prologue, ask students to analyze the characterization of Antigone and her sister Ismene. What problem does Antigone report to her sister. What does Antigone intend to do? What is Ismene's reaction to this intention? What is Ismene's view of the relationship between men and women? How far is Antigone willing to go for her loved one? Why does Antigone, implying an oxymoron, say that she will "do holy things criminally" when she refers to her proposed deed? What conflict of values is represented in this phrase?

• Examine Creon's first long speech in which he outlines the philosophy that guides his actions and his edict. What human institution does Creon believe to be most important in life? Compare his beliefs with those of Antigone. On what specific points does Creon contradict Antigone?

• Make a list of man's civilized skills as enumerated by the Chorus. According to the Chorus, is there any limitation to man's mastery of nature? Does it view man's cleverness as unambiguously "wondrous" or is there something "terrible" about it? Explain your answer.

• The second episode presents the face-to-face confrontation of the two antagonists, Antigone and Creon. What is the attitude of the Chorus and the Guard with regard to the capture of Antigone? How does Antigone defend her defiance of the edict? How does Antigone view the relationship between laws made by man and those created by the gods? What is Creon's view of the relationship between man and woman and the relative importance of blood ties versus ties of citizenship? How does this contrast with Antigone's view of the same? What is Antigone's attitude with regard to her deed and with regard to Ismene's attempt to share responsibility for the deed?

- How would the Athenian audience have received Creon's statement to his son, Haemon: "It is necessary to obey him whom the city puts in charge even in small matters, whether they are just or unjust"? According to Haemon, what is the reaction of the common people to Creon's decree of death for Antigone? What advice does Haemon give to Creon? What criticisms does Haemon make of Creon? Why does Creon change Antigone's punishment from public stoning to burial alive in a cave? In the end, what has Creon learned about the law? What moral lesson does the Chorus see in the fate of Creon at the close of the play?

Solve a Gender Issue in the Workplace Using the Six-Step Model of the Future Problem Solving Program (FPSP)

Ask each student to record evidence of their team's discussion in their own project log. Divide students into groups of four and use the following scenario as the basis for the six-step problem solving process:

A group of women who all work in the Franklin Glue Factory are sitting around a lunch table talking about the kinds of problems women today encounter in the work force in the year 2015.

- ◆ Identify challenges in the Future Scene. In groups, brainstorm 10 problems/issues that women in the work force would encounter. To generate ideas, FPSP recommends that students consider the following areas: social relationships, business, environmental, education, technology, recreation, government and politics, ethics and religion, arts and aesthetics, physical/health, basic needs, economics, law and justice, communication, and miscellaneous. Each member of the group should write these problems in their project log. See *Brainstorming Problems Women Encounter in the Work Force* for examples of students' brainstorming.

Brainstorming Problems Women Encounter in the Work Force

Problems Women Encounter in the Work Force

1. Sexual harassment

2. Men leaving their own responsibilities for the women to do

3. Promotional discrimination

4. People feeling more comfortable with men in the higher-ranking positions

5. Job separation-men working with their hands; women working in clerical positions

6. Women are more criticized for their mistakes

7. Lower pay for women

8. Women are not as respected for their intelligence and thus have little authority

9. Hostile work environment for women

10. Women are made to feel physically inferior

♦ Determine an Underlying Problem. Each group must rank the problems in order of their importance and identify only one problem that it deems the most important. Students must state the underlying problem using FPSP standard format: (1) condition phrase, (2) stem plus key verb phrase: "how might we…" or "in what ways might we…," (3) purpose for the action in key verb phrase, (4) time, place, topic. Write it as your next log entry (FPSP Coach's Handbook, p. 107).

Student example: Because women receive fewer promotional opportunities in the work force, how might we help them achieve their potential through affirmative action policies in the Franklin Glue Factory by the year 2015.

At this point, students need to research their topic to acquire accurate information using at least five resources (two journal articles, two news articles, three Internet Web sites).

♦ Produce Solution Ideas to the Underlying Problem. After identifying and researching the one most important problem, each team member must generate 10 possible solutions to that one problem. See *Solution Ideas for Women's Limited Promotion Opportunities* on page 134.

Solution Ideas for Women's Limited Promotion Opportunities

1. Promotional board should have an equal number of men and women

2. The most qualified person for the job should be hired regardless of sex

3. Omit gender from application forms

4. Seniority should rule

5. If women are the minority, they need to be considered for minority rights

6. Women should not back down when discriminated against and should take appropriate action

7. If denied promotion the first time, women should get the promotion without question the next time it is offered

8. Women should be given legitimate reasons for being turned down for a promotion

9. Women should investigate their equal opportunity rights under the law

10. There should be an equal number of men and women eligible for the job

♦ Generate and Select Criteria to Evaluate Solution Ideas. Next, each group should generate at least five criteria to evaluate their solution ideas. They might consider criteria such as cost, legal rights, practicality, equality, desirability, etc. When the group comes to consensus on evaluation criteria, each member should next rank the solutions and record them in their project logs.

♦ Evaluate Solution Ideas to Determine the Better Action Plan. Each group should come to consensus and write the best solution in their project logs. For instance, here is the student sample for the above group:

Best: The most qualified person regardless of gender should be offered the promotion.

♦ Develop an Action Plan. Using their best solution, students are now ready to develop an action plan to promote their solution. Encourage students to imagine realistic ways to implement their solution. This plan might include legal action, public awareness, or other make-a-difference projects. See *FPSP Assessment Criteria for the Project Log* on page 136, which culminates in the action plan taken from FPSP Coach's Handbook (2000, pp. 185–186) and FPSP Evaluation Primer (2000, pp. 89–98).

Assessment of the Group Process

Ask each group to document what it has learned about working in a group setting and about the nature of the problem with which the group has dealt. Groups should provide reflective comments, as well as conference with the teacher concerning their individual participation in the group. See *Students' Reflective Comments* on page 137 and *Assessment Rubric for Individual Participation in the Group Problem-Solving Process* on page 138.

Expository Essays

Students write an expository piece based on reading and class discussion of Antigone, on the work done by the group, and on their own personal opinion. See *Assessment Rubric for Expository Essay* on page 139.

FPSP Assessment Criteria for the Project Log

	1	2	3	4	5
Relevance— the action plan's relation to the underlying problem	The action plan does not address the underlying problem	The action plan has some relation to the underlying problem; another solution might be better	The action plan relates to the underlying problem but needs more elaboration	The action plan does a good job of addressing the underlying problem	The action plan is very relevant to the underlying problem
Effectiveness— the action plan's effectiveness in solving the underlying problem	The action plan does little to solve the underlying problem	The action plan barely addresses the underlying problem	The action plan attempts to solve the underlying problem	The action plan adequately solves the underlying problem; plan is elaborated	The action plan creatively solves the underlying problem and has detailed explanation
Impact—the plan's impact on the future scene	The action plan has little effect on the future scene; underlying problem scored low in adequacy	Effect on the future scene is not strong; underlying problem may vary in adequacy	The plan attempts to impact the future scene; underlying problem may vary in adequacy	The plan has effect on the future scene; underlying problem of average adequacy	The plan has a strong, positive impact on the future scene; underlying problem high in adequacy
Humaneness— the positive, humane potential of the plan	Negative or destructive action plan	Action plan is neutral-neither positive nor negative	Positive potential exists in the action plan	Action plan is humane for the most part, but needs to be more assertive	Action plan is practical, positive, and constructive
Development of action plan—the degree to which the team explains its plan	The action plan fails to describe the obstacles that need to be overcome in the underlying problem	The action plan needs additional details to make the plan more complete in addressing the underlying problem	The action plan addresses some but not all of the issues stated in the underlying problem	The action plan shows a modest way of solving the underlying problem	The action plan shows a new, creative way of solving the underlying problem
Research Applied—evidence of research in the project log	No research evident	Minimal demonstration of research, terms, etc.	Shows limited knowledge of topic; more research possible	Research noticeable in challenges, solutions, and action plan	Research readily apparent in challenges, solutions, and action plan
Creative Strength— creativity of project log	Log has stereotypical ideas	Log has traditional ideas rather than innovative ideas	Evidence of innovative thinking	Creative thinking, fresh insights; Log goes beyond the ordinary	Strong display of inventive, ingenious ideas
Futuristic Thinking— futuristic ideas contained in the log	Log shows no understanding of how ideas impact the future	Log shows little understanding of how ideas impact the future	Log shows basic understanding of how ideas impact the future	Log shows good understanding of how ideas impact the future	Log does excellent job of tying ideas to futuristic concepts

Total Points

Grade Scale

Students' Reflective Comments

- I realized how much discrimination still exists in the work force.
- I learned how easily discrimination can be eliminated.
- Equal opportunities never really exist.
- Company policies on discrimination are generally ignored or unsuccessful.
- I learned how important compromise is.
- I learned how to set goals and achieve them within the framework of a group setting.
- It is easier to solve problems in a group discussion.
- Most issues directly affect the genders differently.
- There are many diverse opinions and solutions.

Assessment Rubric for Individual Participation in the Group Problem-Solving Process

Exemplary (4)	*Adequate (3)*	*Minimal (2)*	*Unacceptable (1)*
• Weighs multiple perspectives on an issue and considers the good	• Demonstrates knowledge of important ideas related to an issue	• Makes statements about the issue that express only personal attitude	• Remains silent or contributes no thoughts of her or his own
• Uses relevant knowledge to analyze an issue	• States an issue for the group to consider and presents more than one viewpoint	• Mentions a potentially important idea but does not pursue it in a way that advances the group's understanding	• Makes only irrelevant comments
• Employs a higher order discussion strategy such as argument by analogy, stipulation, or resolution	• Supports a position with reasons or evidence		• Makes no comments that facilitate dialogue.
• Engages in more than one sustained interchange or summarizes and assesses the progress of the discussion.	• Engages in an extended interchange with at least one other person	• Invites contributions implicitly or explicitly	• Makes comments that are primarily negative in character.
• Makes no comments that inhibit others' contributions and intervenes if others do this.	• Paraphrases important statements as a transition or summary	• Responds constructively to ideas expressed by at least one other person	
	• Asks another person for an explanation or clarification germane to the discussion	• Tends not to make negative statements	
	• Does not inhibit others' contributions		

Assessment Rubric for Expository Essay

	Exemplary (4)	Adequate (3)	Minimal (2)	Unacceptable (1)
Content	Focuses on the topic, clearly addresses the purpose, has vivid supporting details	Relates to the topic, generally addresses the purpose, and has adequate supporting details	Demonstrates an awareness of the topic, but may include extraneous or loosely related material; demonstrates an attempt to address the purpose and includes some supporting details	Is only slightly related to the topic and offers few supporting details; may or may not attempt to address the purpose
Organization	Has a logical organizational pattern that demonstrates a sense of flow and conveys a sense of completeness and wholeness	Has a logical order that demonstrates a sense of flow and a sense of wholeness and completeness, although some lapses may occur	Shows an attempt at an organizational pattern, but exhibits little sense of flow or completeness	Has little evidence of organization; thoughts are randomly linked together
Language/ Audience Awareness/ Style	Uses language effectively by exhibiting word choices that are appropriate to the subject, purpose, and intended audience; varies writing style according to purpose	Includes word choices that are appropriate to the subject, purpose, and intended audience; generally varies writing style according to purpose	Has limited and predictable vocabulary and makes word choices which may not show an awareness of audience, purpose, or subject; contains an attempt to vary writing style according to purposes	Has limited or inappropriate vocabulary that obscures meaning; shows little or no attempt to vary writing style according to purpose
Sentence Structure	Includes sentences of varied length and structure and exhibits the use of complete sentences except where purposeful phrases or clauses are used for effect	For the most part, exhibits the use of complete sentences except where purposeful phrases or clauses are used for effect; some errors in sentence structure may occur, but they do not impede communication	Contains errors in structure and usage that limit its readability	Demonstrates little knowledge of basic punctuation, capitalization, and spelling of commonly used words
Mechanics	Demonstrates correct usage, punctuation, capitalization, and correctly spells commonly used words	Follows the conventions of usage, punctuation, and capitalization, and correctly spells commonly used words; any errors that occur do not impede communication	Demonstrates some knowledge of capitalization, punctuation, and spelling of commonly used words	Contains errors in sentence structure and usage that impede readability

Bibliography

Future Problem Solving Program, Inc. (2000). *FPSP Coach's Handbook. (2000).* Lexington, KY: Author.

Kiner, C. S., & Hume, K. C. (2000). *Future problem solving program: Evaluation primer.* Lexington, KY: Future Problem Solving Program, Inc.

Ritt, M. (Director). (1979). *Norma Rae* [VHS]. Starring Sally Field.

Wolff, V. E (1993). *Make lemonade.* New York: Henry Holt and Co.

12

THE
I-SEARCH PAPER

Colleen Ruggieri

All men by nature desire knowledge.

Aristotle

Overview of Authentic Learning

In 1984, Ken Macrorie introduced the idea that the research paper could take the form of a first-person narrative he called the "I-Search Paper." Unlike a typical "research" paper, in which students search for something that someone has already searched, this paper allows them to find out for themselves what it is that they need to know. Students choose a burning question/issue that they want to learn more about. They utilize all of our available resources to answer their questions, including the library (books, periodicals, newspapers), and the Internet. In addition to these types of sources, students need to seek out an "expert" on their subject matter and interview her/him-either in person, or on the phone. Students write the story of their search in chronological order in first person, documenting their sources, as they proceed on the journey. The strength of this project is that the students' research process is captured and valued, in contrast to assessment of a final product, as in the traditional research paper. When students' questions are answered and they are satisfied with the results, they write a self-reflection paper describing their research process and their growth as a reader/researcher/writer/thinker. The student examples for this assessment are taken from the "I-Search Paper" written by Ashlee Russo, Boardman High School, Youngstown, Ohio.

NCTE/IRA Standards

In this assessment, students will:

♦ Choose a topic for their I-Search Paper, reflect on their prior knowledge, and describe their interest in researching the topic. In doing so, students will participate as knowledgeable, reflective, creative, and critical members of a variety of literacy communities (NCTE/IRA Standard #11).

♦ Research the topic using print, nonprint, Internet, and interview resources. In doing so, students will read a wide range of print and nonprint texts to acquire new information; to respond to the needs and demands of society and the workplace; and for personal fulfillment (NCTE/IRA Standard #1); students will apply a wide range of strategies to comprehend, interpret, evaluate, and appreciate texts. They will draw on their prior experience, their interactions with other readers and writers, their knowledge of word meaning and of other texts, their word identification strategies, and their understanding of textual features (NCTE/IRA Standard #3); students will conduct research on issues and interests by generating ideas and questions, and by posing problems. They will gather, evaluate, and synthesize data from a variety of sources to communicate their discoveries in ways that suit their purpose and audience (NCTE/IRA Standard #7); and, students will use a variety of technological and informational resources to gather and synthesize information and to create and communicate knowledge (NCTE/IRA Standard #8).

♦ Reflect on their research, thinking, and learning processes. In doing so, students will use spoken, written, and visual language to accomplish their own purposes (NCTE/IRA Standard #12).

Sketch of I-Searching for Students (Macrorie pp. 62–63)

♦ Once you've got a topic, take it to class or the group you're working with, tell the others how you became interested in it, and ask them if they can help you-tips, names, addresses, phone numbers of experts, whatever is useful.

♦ Find experts or authorities. Ask them where to locate the most useful books, magazines, newspapers, films, tapes, or other experts on your topic.

♦ Look at or listen to this information and these ideas. Note and write down what may be useful to you.

♦ Before you interview people who know a lot about your topic, think about the best way to approach them. Through another person who knows them? Directly, by telephone, or by letter? Find out what their lives are like. When would they be most apt to have time and inclination to talk to you? Do you need an introduction of some sort from others?

♦ If you're largely ignorant on the topic you're going to ask them about, they may resent your taking up their time, because they will probably get less than you do from an exchange. Know something of the topic before you talk to them.

♦ If you're worried that experts may not be able to spare you time, begin by asking them where you might look for information and advice on your topic. Then, if they don't want to talk at length with you, or don't have time, they can refer you to others.

♦ Test the statements of experts against those of other experts.

♦ Consult both firsthand sources (people who talk to you about what they're doing, or objects and events you observe on your own) and secondhand sources (books, magazines, newspapers, or people who tell you about what others have done). Remember that experts are persons who know a lot about something. They need not hold an official position or be a certain age.

Form

The paper will be divided into four main parts (Macrorie, p. 64):

Part I: What I Know (and didn't know about my topic when I started out).

Part II: Why I'm Writing This Paper. (Here's where a real need should show up: the writer demonstrates that the search may make a difference in her/his life).

Part III: The Search (story of the hunt).

Part IV: What I Learned (or didn't learn-a search that failed can be as exciting and valuable as one that succeeded).

Documentation

In addition to citing references within the story, create a Works Cited page at the end of your paper. Your language and style should belong to you. As you think of your search and topic, maybe you feel formal or informal—it makes no difference. Write the way that seems natural, as long as you don't write in "Engfish"—Macrorie's definition for the "say-nothing, feel-nothing, word-wasting, pretentious language of traditional schools" (p. 22).

Required Sources

   (2) books

   (3) periodicals (magazines/newspapers)

   (2) Internet articles

   (1) interview

Some Notes on Sources

Internet

Realize that just because there is a Web site for a topic, that does not necessarily mean that it is a good one. Review the endings in *Internet Sources* to determine the source of your material from the Internet.

	Internet Sources
.com	commercial site
.edu	educational institution
.gov	government agency or dept.
.mil	military organization
.org	other type of organization; usually not nonprofit
.firm	businesses
.store	online stores
.web	Web-related organizations
.arts	cultural and entertainment organizations
.info	organizations that provide information
.nom	individuals who want to be identified as such

You will also want to consider whether or not the Web site is an accurate, authoritative source for your information. An individual's homepage might be enlightening, but you must consider whether or not the person is credible.

Interview

Realize that your person should be an "expert" on your subject area. A teacher might be a good person to approach for a question about education, whereas your friend might be a good person to ask if he or she has had life experiences in the area that you are investigating.

Books

Check the publication dates-older materials may provide you with outdated information.

Performance Tasks

See *Finding the "Burning Question" for the" I-Search Paper"* on page 146 for a worksheet to help scaffold students' thinking about an issue that concerns them.

Parts I and II: What I know, What I Want to Know, and Why I Want to Know It

When beginning the paper, students should be clear as to why they are searching for a particular answer. In this section, students might include: a list of questions they hope to answer at the end of their search, an explanation of the dialectic elements, what they already know, and what theories they already have. In addition, this section should include what students hope to find out, why they are interested in the topic, what they hope to gain from the search, people they know who connect them to the search, experiences the students have that connected them to the search, and things that they have seen or read about the topic (minimum of 200 words). See excerpt of *Ashlee's Binge Drinking: What Do I Need To Know and Why Am I Interested?* on page 147.

Finding the "Burning Question" for the "I-Search Paper"

On the lines below, list five items that really matter to you-these may be people, interests/hobbies, things, concerns, etc.

1. _____

2. _____

3. _____

4. _____

5. _____

Now that you have listed these five things, think of five burning questions that you have about these things-unresolved conflicts, ideas, curiosities, etc. Write the questions on the lines below.

1. _____

2. _____

3. _____

4. _____

5. _____

As you look at these questions, consider which one is the most important to you right now. Which one do you think might most inspire you and make you want to find the answer(s)? Once you have selected your question, you have taken the first step in beginning our next composition, the I-Search paper. During the next eight weeks, we will work together to polish your writing skills and to discover the answers that you are seeking.

Binge Drinking: What Do I Need
to Know and Why Am I Interested?

Parts I and II

Binge drinking is something that goes on at every college in every town. It is a very serious problem that plagues many college students. Since I am only a few years away from graduating from high school, I find great interest in college students and their lives. Usually when the word "college" is brought up, most high school students think of partying all night and drinking. My quest is to find out why drinking heavily to the point of vomiting, passing out, and possibly going to the hospital or dying is considered something "fun" or "cool."

My interest in this topic was first captured by an event that occurred when I was in eighth grade. A high school student in my community died in a car accident that resulted from his drunk driving. The smashed car was placed in front of the high school, which led me to ask myself why so many kids put themselves in danger just to have one night of fun. Recently, my cousin, a college student, crashed his car after drinking and becoming intoxicated from a large amount of alcohol. He was never the type of kid to get involved with drinking, but college life seemed to change that. I have read many articles in magazines and stories of tragedies in newspapers that have dealt with binge drinking. I am personally looking for a reason as to why some kids choose to drink so heavily.

I have a few theories of my own that deal with why college students binge drink. I believe that kids drink because so many others are doing it. It seems like the cool thing to do. I wonder, though, why people think it's cool to pass out or vomit. I also theorize that young adults drink because it makes them feel as if they are accepted. What they don't know is how they are putting their lives in danger. Perhaps they do know this important fact, but choose to ignore it. Maybe students drink to "hide" their identities and be more relaxed and comfortable with themselves. Hopefully, my search will lead to me to the facts I need to validate some of my assumptions.

A psychologist may be very helpful in my search. There are yet a few final questions for which I would like answers: What exactly is considered binge drinking? What gender typically drinks more? How often is

there unwanted sexual intercourse after drinking? What kinds of students become binge drinkers? Most importantly, what is it about binge
drinking that makes it seem cool? Hopefully, finding the answers will
steer me away from making wrong choices and binge drinking in college.
     The search begins....

Part III: The Search

In part three, students will be reflecting on the journey of the search. They
will use "I" often, because they will be taking the reader through the search
with them. While students are searching, they will record their notes in a journal. Each day that students do anything for the paper—stop at the library, read
an article, try to call someone—they should note it in their journals. This journal
can be handwritten or computer-generated, and it should also highlight the student's emotional state and personal observations made while writing. They
could indicate happiness at finding something, frustration and rising stress if
something goes wrong, etc. Each journal entry should be dated and should
indicate their location, type of media or person they are interviewing, and what
they are asking, thinking, and finding. As far as Macrorie is concerned, when
the student has answered her/his questions and summarized the important
findings, the "I-Search Paper" is complete. The journal tells the story of the
search in informal language. However, if you require students to write a traditional research paper, students could take the information from their I-Search
Papers and transpose it to the formal essay format. See *Excerpts from Ashlee's
Search on Binge Drinking.*

Excerpts from Ashlee's Search on Binge Drinking

Part III

May 20—In the school library

*When young adults talk about "six packs," are they talking about good look-
ing abdomen muscles or cans of Bud Light? While a few fitness buffs might
be referring to flat stomachs, the reality is that most college students are referring to alcohol and lots of it. It seems as if even students who should
know better are tempted to hit the bottle during the college years. In the library, I found a great article in USA Today by researcher Linda Temple on
page 67, who provides insight into the issue: "85 percent of the students*

said that when they find themselves surrounded by drinkers, they ignore the warnings they've been pummeled with since childhood."

She also points her finger at College bookstores that often promote alcohol by selling beer mugs and shot glasses decorated with school mascots and crests. In addition to the environmental surroundings, students are also influenced by the lure of doing something that makes them feel older. According to Temple, "sixty percent of students carry fake ideas with them, though most of them will say that they are not even necessary when going to establishments that serve alcohol." Despite all of the dangers of binge drinking, college students around the world still do not understand all of the risks. From football games to spring break, alcohol is everywhere. Temple explains that consequences of drinking on college campuses could be anything from written warnings to alcohol counseling, but it is rare for a student to ever be expelled or ousted from a dorm as a result of consuming alcohol. I can already see that the consequences are not severe enough to deter drinking in college.

May 23-Interview with my cousin, Josh Russo

Although some people say that binge drinking is directly related to peer pressure, Josh said that drinking has nothing to do with this: "No one really cares who drinks and who doesn't." According to him, he and other students drink merely because "they like it." He said that "Everyone likes it and until alcohol doesn't get anyone drunk, everyone is going to do it." Of course that day won't ever come! When I asked him if he knew how dangerous binge drinking can be for a person's health and well being, he offered a simple reply: "Ah, I know my limits." Ironically, this student went on to flip his car during a drunk driving accident. I think his attitude is typical of many students. They think that they are indestructible; the reality is that most do not understand the dangers associated with drinking. Maybe I should ask Ms. Burns what she thinks about it.

May 24—Interview with Dr. Marilyn Burns, Psychologist

Dr. Burns just confirmed what Josh told me about why students engage in binge drinking. She said, "Kids drink because their friends do. They're curious about how they'll feel if they're drunk. Kids think that they'll lose friends or won't be popular if they don't drink." Peer pressure seems to be the main culprit, in spite of what Josh said that students drink because they like the drink. It's probably a lot like smoking. You have to do it to belong to the group.

May 26—At home on the internet

My question tonight is why does college social life revolve so heavily around drinking?

At the Harvard University publications site, I found that the college setting seems in many ways to influence students when it comes to the consumption of alcohol. At the Screen 1 of the President, research shows that students drink because they get the impression that it is acceptable from their roommates who stay up with them every night when they're drunk and from administrators who accommodate the drinking of students. This site goes on to say that once students choose to drink, there are a large number of problems and consequences that go along with the decision. Missing classes, getting into arguments, having unplanned or unprotected sex, getting into trouble with campus and local police, and driving drunk are all potential problems associated with drinking. Other problems reported by non-drinkers include: dealing with property damage, babysitting roommates, having sleep interrupted and experiencing an unwanted sexual advance. The effects of alcohol, therefore, not only affect those consuming the alcohol, but also the nondrinkers around them. It seems as if college life often revolves around dealing with the consequences of alcohol consumption.

May 28—At the library reading a microfiche of the New York Times

Once students choose to drink, there are a number of problems that happen. According to Hitt, thirty percent of binge drinkers reported in engaging in unplanned, and probably unprotected sexual activity. He tells the story about his nephew, a junior in college, which explained a typical party-goer's schedule: drive off campus somewhere or hide in the woods to drink, eat a box of breath mints, and go to a party." His nephew continued the habit even though his nephew knew two students who fell off a cliff as a result of alcohol poisoning, and five others who were hurt or even paralyzed in car accidents after episodes of binge drinking.

May 29—In the library reading "Party Politics" in The New Republic

I've been looking for something that would explain why kids would continue to drink in spite of so much tragedy. This article only confirms the dangers of drinking. For example, Adam Herringa, a 22-year-old graduate of MSU, led a protest of 3,000 students against a ban on alcohol at tailgating parties. In April of 1998, University of Connecticut students quarreling with police set fires and vandalized twenty-seven police cars during a weekend of partying. According to the Center for Science in Public Interest, in the past year and a half, eighteen students died as a result of alcohol related accidents such as falling out of windows, falling down stairs, falling into rivers, and choking on vomit. These tragedies all focused around excessive intake of alcohol. Even knowing that death is a possible consequence of consuming alcohol does not seem to curb such behavior.

June 1—In library reading a book by Elaine Landau called
Teenage Drinking

I continue to search for reasons why students engage in binge drinking in spite of the tragic consequences. Here is an incident about binge drinking at Princeton University. Thirty-nine fraternity pledges ended up at the school infirmary and local hospital after they completed an initiation ceremony in which students were blindfolded and liquor was poured down their throats: "One of the students remained in a coma for over twenty- four hours" (14). When asked why they drank at parties, many responded that alcohol made them "feel free" and gave them a chance to be themselves (43). I do not think that college students understand the risk they are taking when they consume alcohol. I'm sure that when I am in college, I am going to have a few drinks, but because I am aware of the dangers, I won't do binge drinking when I get to college.

Part IV: What I Learned (or Didn't Learn)

At the end of the project, ask students to reflect on their research, learning, and thinking skills. What new skills did they learn in the process? What did they learn about your subject? What did they learn about themselves? How did they handle deadlines? How well did they work independently? How did they ultimately feel about what they discovered (minimum 300 words)? See excerpts form Ashlee's self-reflection on *What I Learned,* on page 152, and *Assessment Rubric for the "I Search" Paper* on page 154.

What I Learned

Part IV

Stressed out, frustrated, relieved, excited and nervous. These are all feelings that I experienced throughout the I-Search paper. I've never done a research paper quite like this one before, and I certainly learned a great deal about a variety of things—finding and analyzing information about the topic of binge drinking, learning how to format a paper, and dealing with deadlines and pressure. I enjoyed learning about drinking, but there were times when I felt so overwhelmed that I wanted to scream. Binge drinking, I discovered through my research, is very harmful. I truly believe that students do not understand the risk that they are taking when they consume alcohol. I'm sure that when I am in college I am going to have a few drinks, but because I am aware of the dangers, I don't believe that I will exceed a few drinks a night.

I felt that I handled the deadlines well. Every day I worked a little harder on my paper. Honestly, I have never worked as much on one report as I did on the I-Search. When some students told me that their report was eight pages long, I wanted to cry. Now, however, the contents of my report suit me, even if it isn't as long as some of the other papers. I finally figured out one of my worst habits: I am a procrastinator. I like to think that I will do everything tomorrow. Then tomorrow turns into the next day. It is truly an awful habit, but I am aware of it now and can improve upon myself.

Everyone that played a part in my research is deserving of my thanks. Ms. Burns is a sweetheart; she was very nice to me. My cousin, Josh, provided me with a lot of help. I feel that he helped me to make connections when comparing the research with real life. I feel bad for my mom because she had to listen to me read the paper over and over again. The I-Search made me think about my friends as well, and wonder who among them will go on to become binge drinkers. I never thought anything of it before, but a lot of my friends drink, and this seriously worries me now.

The I-Search made me think a lot about myself. I know now that I am the type of person who will try to succeed and be the best in every possible way. When our class first began the I-Search, I was ready to work my tail off to make my paper a good one. Even though I still might make errors in mechanics or citations, I am satisfied with my efforts. I know that I no longer want to be the kind of person who puts everything off until the last second and then struggles to finish the work. I have also learned that if something doesn't work out while I'm doing something, I can find something better if I keep searching.

Thank you, Mrs. Ruggieri, for giving me this opportunity to learn about life, my friends, and myself. This was a worthwhile experience that has made me more aware, a little wiser, and even prouder. The I-Search seemed to be an awful assignment in the beginning, but in the end it became an assignment that allowed me to grow and gain from it.

Bibliography

Macrorie, K. (1988). *The I-search paper: Revised edition of searching writing.* Portsmouth, NH: Boynton/Cook Publishers.

Assessment Rubric for the "I-Search Paper"

	Superior Paper (4 Points)	*Very Good Paper (3 Points)*	*Average Paper (2 Points)*	*Below Average (1 Point)*
Critical Thinking Skills	The paper contains evidence of strong critical thinking skills directed toward answering a question and solving a problem	The paper contains evidence of very good critical thinking skills directed toward answering a question and solving a problem	The paper contains evidence of average critical thinking skills directed toward answering a question and solving a problem	The paper shows no or few critical thinking skills directed toward answering a question and solving a problem
Research	The paper is validated by a wide range of sources that demonstrate sound research efforts. Internet, periodical, book, and interview sources are all utilized and presented without errors according to MLA standards	The paper is validated by a fairly wide range of sources that demonstrate sound research efforts. Internet, periodical, book, and interview sources are all utilized and presented with minimal errors according to MLA standards	The paper is validated by a minimum range of sources that demonstrate sound research efforts. Internet, periodical, book, and interview sources are all utilized and presented with minimal errors according to MLA standards	The paper is not validated by sources that demonstrate sound research efforts. Internet, periodical, book, and interview sources are not utilized and presented correctly according to MLA standards
Support for Ideas	All of the main ideas of the paper are well supported with specific examples	Most of the main ideas of the paper are well supported with examples	The main ideas of the paper are supported with minimal examples	The main ideas of the paper are not supported with examples
Personal Growth and Knowledge	The paper clearly indicates an outstanding level of personal growth and knowledge gained through the writing process	The paper clearly indicates a good level of personal growth and knowledge gained through the writing process	The paper indicates a minimal level of personal growth and knowledge gained through the writing process	The paper indicates a lack of personal growth and indicates that little knowledge has been gained through the writing process
Language/ Audience	Language used in the paper is appropriate to audience and topic	Language used in the paper is almost always appropriate to audience and topic	Language used in the paper is fairly appropriate to audience and topic	Language used in the paper is often inappropriate to audience and topic
Conventions	The paper exhibits solid mastery of language structure, conventions, and figurative language and is free of errors	The paper exhibits solid mastery of language structure, conventions, and figurative language, and contains only minimal errors	The paper lacks a solid mastery of language structure, conventions, and figurative language, and contains errors	The paper lacks a solid mastery of language structure, conventions, and figurative language, and contains several errors

13

PORTFOLIO OF THREATS AND SOLUTIONS TO THE ENVIRONMENT

Jacqueline Glasgow

Education: a debt due from present to future generations.

George Peabody

The environmental crisis is the greatest challenge of our times. Since the dropping of the nuclear bomb on Hiroshima on August 6, 1945, and the development of nuclear weapons around the globe that followed, other threats to the environment have emerged. We suffer the results of poisons in the air from industrial advancements, chemical toxins that are saturating our soil and water, and the threat of radiation and nuclear wastes whether we use the atomic nucleus for energy or war. The Persian Gulf War of 1991 was an environmental war that began with a struggle over the fossil fuel, oil, which is at the root of so many environmental evils. In *Our Angry Earth,* Asimov and Pohl (1991) provide a clear and understandable picture of the current state of our planet, based on recent scientific information. They asked the question, "Can we hope that the world will somehow recover from the environmental harm we do?" (p. 11). They believe it can happen. "There can be a happy ending to it all… if we have the wisdom and the willingness to make it happen, by doing some pretty difficult things" (p. xii). O'Brien's *Z for Zachariah* is an excellent Young Adult novel to teach along with this unit because its main character, sixteen-year-old Anne

Burden, manages to survive a nuclear war sheltered in a protected valley. The book shows both survival in a ruined world and a human element, the importance of moral relationships.

Overview of Authentic Learning

During this unit, students will begin by making a collaborative class project, an Environment Letter Book based on the concepts presented in Our Angry Earth, to provide students with fundamental concepts about the environment. They will research and write a position paper on the pros and cons of organic farming or genetic altering of foods. The unit concludes by asking students to create a portfolio on a current threat and solution to the environment, complete with a personal action plan to make a difference in protecting our earth.

NCTE/IRA Standards

During this unit, students will:

- Learn vocabulary regarding the environment. In doing so, students whose first language is not English make use of their first language to develop competency in the English language arts and to develop understanding of content across the curriculum.

- Conduct research into a current threat to the environment. In doing so, students will read a wide range of print and nonprint texts to acquire new information; to respond to the needs and demands of society, using nonfiction works (NCTE/IRA Standard #1); students will read a wide range of literature in many genres to build an understanding of the many dimensions of human experience (NCTE/IRA Standard #2); and students will conduct research on issues and interests by generating ideas and questions, and by posing problems. They will gather, evaluate, and synthesize data from a variety of sources (e.g., print and nonprint texts, artifacts, people) to communicate their discoveries in ways that suit their purpose and audience (NCTE/IRA Standard #7).

- Develop "Technocures" (solutions) to the problems. In doing so, students will apply a wide range of strategies to comprehend, interpret, evaluate, and appreciate texts (NCTE/IRA Standard #3), and students will conduct research on issues and interests by generating ideas and questions, and by posing problems. They will gather, evaluate, and synthesize data from a variety of sources (e.g., print and nonprint texts, artifacts, people) to communicate their discoveries in ways that suit their purpose and audience, (NCTE/IRA Standard #7) and students will use a variety of technological and informational resources (e.g., libraries, databases, computer networks, videos) to gather and synthesize information and to create and communicate knowledge (NCTE/IRA Standard #8).

- Design a nonelectric home and survival plan. In doing so, students will use spoken, written, and visual language to accomplish their own purposes (NCTE/IRA Standard #12).

- Write a position paper and give a presentation on the pros and cons of organic farming practices or genetically altered food. In doing so, students will adjust their use of spoken, written, and visual language to communicate effectively with a variety of audiences and for different purposes (NCTE/IRA Standard #4); they will employ a wide range of strategies as they write and use different writing process elements appropriately to communicate with different audiences for a variety of purposes (NCTE/IRA Standard #5); they will apply knowledge of language structure, language conventions, media techniques, figurative language, and genre to create, critique, and discuss print and nonprint texts (NCTE/IRA Standard #6); and students will use spoken, written, and visual language to accomplish their own purposes (NCTE/IRA Standard #12).

- Design a Personal Action Plan. In doing so, students will participate as knowledgeable, reflective, creative, and critical members of a variety of literacy communities (NCTE/IRA Standard #11).

Performance Tasks for the Environment Letter Book

In Z for Zachariah (1987), Ann Burden learned her ABC's from a picture book called The Bible Letter Book (p.74). This book combined pictures with letters to help children learn their letters along with important people and places in the Bible. It began with "A" for Adam and ended with "Z" for Zachariah (p.75). Although this book serves a prophetic purpose in O'Brien's novel, it also serves as a model for learning vocabulary relevant to this unit. Ask students to make a class book entitled, The Environment Letter Book, by selecting terms in *Vocabulary for The Environment Letter Book* on page 158. Most of these terms are found in Assimov and Pohl's (1991) Our Angry Earth.

Each student should select at least one term so that all the letters of the alphabet are represented. Students are to define the term(s), give examples, and create an illustration for it. The students should research who or what the topic is; when and why it was important; and what its impact is on the environment or on our society today. Illustrations can be drawings, paintings, clip art, Internet images, photos, or magazine pictures. The student's entry, consisting of text and graphic, should be complete on one page and be ready for insertion into the class book. Make copies for students to learn the vocabulary or leave the class book for reference during this unit. See *Model Page for the Environment Letter Book* on page 158 and *Assessment Rubric for Environment Letter Book* on page 158.

Vocabulary for The Environment Letter Book

Acid rain (p. 76)
Air pollution (p. 76)
Biomass fuel (p. 172)
Carbon dioxide (p. 41)
Carbon monoxide (p. 76)
Chernobyl (p. 79)
Chlorofluorocarbons (p. 39)
Deforestation (p. 138)
Doolittle (p. 21)
Dyson (p. 41)
Electromagnetic energy (p. 184)
Fossil fuels (p. 189)
Fusion power (p. 177)
Gaia hypothesis (p.13)
Geothermal energy (p. 178)
Greenhouse effect (p. 39)

Green revolution (p. 147)
Hanford Nuclear Reservation (p.145)
Homeostasis (p. 15)
Irrigation (p. 235)
Jamaica (p. 58)
Kinetic energy (p. 182)
Kyshtym (p.79)
Laterite soil (p. 137)
Lovelock, James (p.13)
Methane (p. 43)
Nitrogen (p. 77)
Nitrous oxide (p. 39)
Organic waste (p. 238)
Ozone (p. 76)
Photovoltaics (p. 185)
Radiation poisoning (p. 79)
Radioactive wastes (p. 145)

Radionuclides (p. 79)
Salmonella poisoning (p. 150)
Sanitary landfills (p. 144)
Solar power (p. 180)
Space pollution (p. 155)
Three Mile Island (p. 172)
Toxic chemicals (p. 78)
Ultraviolet radiation (p. 92)
Uranium carbide (p. 177)
Venice (p. 153)
Vinyl chloride (p. 115)
Water problems (p. 112)
X-ray (p. 161)
Yenisei (p. 124)
Zero population growth (p. 20,28)
Zinc (p. 128)

Model Page for the Environment Letter Book

Genetically Modified Foods

Plants that were given a new gene, changing the DNA in the plant. Examples of foods or food products that have such altered genes include: Papayas, Soybeans, Potatos, Squash, Tomatos, Frito-Lay Fritos Corn Chips, Post Blueberry Morning Cereal, Heinz 2 Baby Cereal, Ultra Slim Fast, Garden Burger, Old El Paso Taco Shells, Alpo Dry Pet Food.

Assessment Rubric for Environment Letter Book

	Publishable	*Needs Revision*	*Draft*
Definition	Complete, insightful, accurate definition	Incomplete, inaccurate definition	Not enough information to judge
Examples	Clear, appropriate, accurate examples	Unclear, inappropriate, or inaccurate examples	Not enough examples to make your point or no examples offered
Graphic	Creative visual image enhancing understanding of the concept; high technical accomplishment	Visual image is misleading, ambiguous, or low technical quality	Visual image is a poor representation of the concept or there is no graphic offered.

Performance Tasks for Writing a Position Paper on the Pros and Cons of Organic Farming or Genetically Altering Food

The appearance of genetically modified foods (GMF) in the marketplace has resulted in a firestorm of public debate, scientific discussion, and media coverage. A variety of ecological and human health concerns come with the new advances made possible by genetic modification. Ask students: "Would you eat genetically modified food? Would you plant it in your garden? What have you heard about genetically modified food? What do you know about organic gardening? Which agricultural method works best in your geographical area?" Tell students they will be learning about the advantages and disadvantages of genetic engineering of foodstuff and organic versus intensive farming. Students need to have some understanding of genetics. Invite a science teacher to give a brief explanation to the class, if necessary. This lesson is adapted from SCOPE: Genetically Modified Foods in Perspective by Sherry Seethaler and teacher partners found online at http://wise.berkeley.edu/teacher/projects.

- Using a jigsaw approach, assign groups to explore the arguments for or against one agricultural method, either organic farming (crops grown without the use of synthetic [man-made] chemical pesticides, herbicides, or fertilizers), intensive farming (crops produced using synthetic pesticides, fertilizers or herbicides) or genetic engineering of food (plants that were given a new gene that alters the DNA in the plant). Students should also develop a list of foods grown by each method and places where one can buy that food.

- Ask each group or pair of students to prepare posters and short oral presentations to teach their classmates about the evidence in support of their position. As students listen to the presentation, they should take notes on the various positions, and the class should discuss the ideas presented.

- Once students have heard all the evidence for and against each position, ask each student to write a position paper in which they choose the type of agriculture they think should be used in their geographical region. See *Assessment Rubric for Position Paper* on page 160.

Assessment Rubric for Position Paper

Score	Meaning (focus, thesis, support)	Structure (organization, flow)	Language (correct sentences, word choice)	Audience/Style
10	The position paper has a clear thesis that grows out of sufficient background and is supported with convincing evidence	The ideas are clearly organized, with the ideas flowing from the thesis in a logical progression using either inductive or deductive reasoning	The language is vivid with correct sentences and colorful word choice	Anticipated the reader's need for a context; strong confident voice
9	The position paper has an ambiguous thesis or is lacking in convincing support for the position	Ideas are there, but are not fully developed or do not further the thesis	The language is clear with minimal sentence and word errors	Needs to attend to reader's need for information; writer needs a more confident voice
8	The position paper contains the main supporting evidence, but, there is unclear focus and insufficient supporting details	The ideas are not clear, need for more elaboration and support for ideas, and/or the organization needs work	There are appropriate word choices and mostly correct sentences	Needs to address reader's concerns and take a more assertive position
7	The position paper has some ideas, but no clear focus, and lacks details of the main events	Not enough significant ideas from the novel; lacking direction and logical progression	Word choices are limited; there are errors in sentence structure	Position confusing to reader, and writer has weak voice
6	The writing lacks clear focus and support	Jumps around; does not move from one point to another logically	Word choices are inappropriate. There are many incorrect sentences	Weak claims and no writer's voice

Performance Tasks for Portfolio of Current Threats and Solutions to the Environment

For this activity, ask students to create a portfolio on a current threat and solution to the environment, especially in the United States. They can collect clippings and pictures from newspapers, magazines, environmental journals and the internet that describe either threats or solutions to the environment.

Choose a Current Threat to the Environment

Encourage students to focus their portfolio on a particular environmental issue, such as poisons in the air, water, or space. They might focus on the greenhouse effect, industrial or agricultural falloff, smog, acid rain, or nuclear wastes. Another alternative is to study your local watershed. They could choose other issues raised in Our Angry Earth: the "Gaia Hypothesis," rationing destruction, and other less threatening issues, such as destruction of natural forests and rivers, as well as extinction of many attractive animal species.

Suggest Solutions to the Threat

In addition to elucidating the threats to the environment in their portfolio, students must also seek to understand and include the solutions to those problems. Asimov and Pohl discuss the "technocures" in the second part of their book. The "technocures" go beyond the recycling known and practiced by some of the students to include energy diets, effective bookkeepers for fuel prices, vehicle pollution, and fixing the home and farm to be more environmentally benign.

Design a Nonelectric Home

In conjunction with suggestions from Asimov and Pohl, ask students to design a nonelectric home and figure its costs. *Lehman's Non-Electric Catalog*, available online at http://www.lehmanns.com, provides books and products for cooking, gardening, country skills, and self-sufficient living. Although this company generally serves the Amish, there are lessons in their catalog for all of us, if we are serious about preserving the environment. In addition to house designing, students could also plan a garden that would support a family of four for a year. What would they like to eat? How much ground should they till? What would it take to feed the family? What tools would they need to plant the garden? Where would they plant it? What long-range plans for the garden should they think about that would provide other products necessary for comfortable living? Another focus for this section would include aspects of the peaceful atom. Radioisotopes and radiation have many applications in agriculture, food preservation, medicine, science, industry, and research. They greatly improve the day-to-day quality of our lives. How can we preserve the beneficial applications and control the evil ones?

Personal Action Project

Asimov and Pohl asked the question, "How far do you want to go?" They gave us the choice to be a missionary to the unsaved, an organizer, or even a political boss (p. 263). Students can choose from these authors' projects or come up with one of their own. One idea is to research the controversy surrounding the stockpiling of nuclear weapons and to write a publishable essay about this controversy. When students have completed their portfolios, they should present them to the class. They should prepare a visual to enhance the central ideas. Some may use music or other special effects. A PowerPoint Presentation would be especially effective if technology is available and accessible. See *Personal Action Project Ideas from Our Angry Earth,* and *Environment Portfolio Assessment Rubric* on page 163.

Personal Action Project Ideas from *Our Angry Earth*

Missionary Work

♦ Write letters to manufacturers of products you buy (p. 266)

♦ List of ecological New Year's resolutions to send out to family members (p. 268)

♦ Letters to editors of newspapers and magazines about appropriate issues (p. 268)

♦ Letters to decision makers: Congressional Representatives, Zoning Board members, etc. (p. 269)

Organization and Action

♦ Join or start an environmental organization (p. 271)

♦ Develop projects, programs, newsletters, fundraisers, mailing lists (pp. 276–284)

♦ Practical Action and consciousness raising activities (pp. 284–288)

Green Politics

♦ Join or start a political club

♦ Influence national, state, and municipal committees (pp. 297–304)

♦ "Get the vote out" during campaigns and on election day (pp. 304–309)

Environmental Portfolio Assessment Rubric

Sections of Portfolio	Exemplary	Acceptable	Drafting	Beginning
Current Threats (Issues) *Content Graphics Variety of Resources*	Clear articulation of the issue; used multiple resources to build a strong understanding of the problem; creative use of graphics to enhance the text	Good understanding of the issue; used at least three resources for research; used graphics to show the effects of the problem	Communicates a partial understanding of the issue; used one or two resources for research; graphics are low-quality	Communicates a vague or incorrect understanding of the issue; used no resources for research; graphics are sketchy or absent
"Technocures" (Solutions) *Quality Feasibility Creativity Resources*	Well-organized, creative solutions to the issue; used persuasive and feasible arguments, used multiple resources	Good, convincing solutions to the problem adequately articulated; used at least three resources for research	Expresses ideas and arguments using limited details; used only one or two resources	Expresses ideas and arguments with few, if any, details; used no outside resources
Nonelectric Home and Survival Plan *Habitable Feasible Creative Resources*	Creative design of a nonelectric home; the house is feasible; used multiple resources to develop the plan; survival plan is outstanding	Good design of a nonelectric home; the home is habitable and comfortable; used at least three resources to develop the plan; survival is possible	The plan is limited and needs more research; the plan is not feasible or possible as it is designed; survival is not possible	The plan is extremely limited or nonexistent; more research is needed; there is no plan for survival
Personal Action Project *Commitment Quality Making a Difference*	The project is outstanding and will effectively make a contribution toward awareness of, and change toward, the issue	The project is excellent and there is commitment to make a difference in rectifying the issue	The project is limited and needs more commitment and higher quality to make a difference in the issue	The project is ill-devised and needs more attention and commitment to make a difference in the issue
Class Presentation	Exemplary communication of the threats and solutions to the issue; visuals enhanced the presentation; strong evidence of research; demonstrates coherent organization and strong development of ideas	Communicates with appropriate style the threats and solutions to the issue; visuals reinforce the central ideas; adequate evidence of research; demonstrates clear organization; uses details effectively to clarify ideas and arguments	Communicates with limited style the threats and solutions to the issue; visuals are ineffective in conveying the main ideas; inadequate evidence of research; demonstrates confusing organization; details are not convincing	Communication is not effective or clearly researched; visuals are ineffective or missing; ideas are confusing and unclear, the organization is limited and sometimes confusing; details are lacking

Bibliography

Asimov, I., & Pohl, F. (1991). *Our angry earth.* New York: Tom Doherty Associates.

Lehmans non-electric catalogue. One Lehman Circle, P.O. Box 321, Kidron, Ohio 44646-0321, 1998, or online at http://www.lehmans.com.

O'Brien, R. (1987). *Z for Zachariah.* New York: Aladdin Paperbacks, Simon & Schuster, Children's Publishing Division.

Orr, D. W. (1994). *Earth in mind: On education, environment, and the human prospect.* Washington, DC: Island Press.

Seethaler, S. (Spring 2000). *SCOPE: Genetically Modified Foods in Perspective* [Online]. Available: http://wise.berkeley.edu/teacher/projects/lessonPlan.php?id=14.

14

READER-RESPONSE JOURNALS

Tom Flynn and Jacqueline Glasgow

Never deprive someone of hope—it may be all they have.

Anonymous

Overview of Authentic Learning

The most widespread use of journals in the English Language Arts classroom, is the reader-response journal. This journal privileges the expression of "individual voice" and development of identity and self-awareness. This expressive journal focuses on the experiences and emotions of the students as they respond to various texts. Students engage in various types of informal writing: freewriting, prewriting, musings, doodlings, diagrams, notes, and drafting activities. According to Anson and Beach, "students actively explore their knowledge, look for patterns in what they generate, freewrite their way toward useable text, write tentative drafts, critique these drafts and respond to the critiques of others, and revise and edit their early attempts as they slowly move toward an improved, final creation" (1995, p. 10). Reader-response journals place thinking and learning at the center; students are constructing their own knowledge. Reader-response journals require students to create a record of their reading, to be involved in the text and to discover that reading and making meaning is a process. These journals also encourage students to see the connection between their lives and what they read. The benefit for teachers is that it gives them something to work with in improving students' responses to literature.

NCTE/IRA Standards

During this unit students will:

♦ Read a short story, poem, or novel, and write a reader-response in their journals. Students will read a wide range of print and nonprint texts to build an understanding of texts, of themselves, and of the cultures of the U.S. and the world; to acquire new information; to respond to the needs and demands of society and the workplace; and for personal fulfillment (NCTE/IRA Standard #1).

♦ Respond to texts, making associative recollections of their experiences and describing their emotional reactions to the text. In doing so, they will apply a wide range of strategies to comprehend, interpret, evaluate, and appreciate texts. They will draw on their prior experience, their interactions with other readers and writers, their knowledge of word meaning and of other texts, their word identification strategies, and their understanding of textual features (NCTE/IRA Standard #3).

♦ Make focal judgments, and complete one-minute responses to their reading. By so doing, students participate as knowledgeable, reflective, creative, and critical members of a variety of literacy communities (NCTE/IRA Standard #11).

♦ Respond to, and analyze, a poem. In doing so, students use spoken, written, and visual language to accomplish their own purposes (NCTE/IRA Standing Standard #12).

Performance Tasks for Reader-Response Journals

Freewriting

Freewriting is an activity in which you write freely to discover and explore ideas. For many writers, topics become apparent only after they have started writing. The surprises in their writing become topics for them. The ideas obtained through freewriting can be expanded and organized into compositions.

Procedure

♦ After you have read the story, think about the issues, themes, or characters that you have been thinking about since you finished reading the book. If students are having difficulty getting started, here are some prompts devised by Mary Kooy (1992) of the University of British Columbia:

• I was impressed or struck by…

• I noticed that…

• I wonder about…

- I predict…
- Some questions I have…
- I don't understand…
- I now understand why/how/what…
- Something I noticed/appreciate/don't appreciate/wonder about is…
- An interesting word/sentence/thought is…
- This part of the story makes me feel…

- Begin writing on paper or composing at the computer for a 10 to 15 minute period. Write down the ideas as they come into your mind while you are concentrating on this activity. Try not to stop writing or take a break during this time period. Let your thoughts, your impressions, and your feelings about the assignment flow freely, writing down anything that seems related.

- After this is done, reread what you have written and highlight ideas that could become topics. Is there an idea that seems to stand apart from the others, one that is particularly interesting or appealing to you, or one that is repeated frequently? Is there something in your freewriting that sums up your thoughts and feelings? If not, can you sum up what your freewriting is about? If your freewriting did not provide you with one worthwhile idea or if you have an idea but cannot write a lot about it, you will need to do more freewriting.

- Choose one of the ideas, and focus your next freewriting on that idea. Write for another 10 to 15 minutes.

Associative Recollections

Some fiction and poetry will elicit personal associations with people and events from your own life. David Bleich, in his book, *Readings and Feelings: An Introduction to Subjective Criticism* (1975), has said that such associations are the "most complex but most useful form of expressing feelings about literature" because they reveal "perception, affect, associations, relationships," and finally the pattern with which individual readers have organized these for themselves (p. 48). This assignment will encourage you to recollect associations from the book of your choice. This activity was adapted from Milner and Milner (1993).

Procedure

- As you read a story, check evocatively familiar moments in the story.
- When you complete the story, return to your checkpoints and consider past associations evoked by your recent reading. In your journal, record the associative recollections prompted by the two most

powerful reference points in the story. Choose at least one point and begin your recollection with a phrase such as one of the following:

- This character/event reminds me of…
- The words here make me think of…
- This part touches a general memory chord, but it reminds me specifically of…
- The way they interact is just like…

Evoked Response

This journal activity will help you elicit an emotional response from the reading of a book. It was adapted from Milner and Milner (1993).

Procedure

- ◆ After reading the entire book silently, select a passage that especially touched you. Then read the passage aloud into a tape recorder. This provides an excellent record of your reaction to the story.

- ◆ Listen to your taped reading, and, in your journal, record any emotion that surfaces in your voice. You can use the following questions to help clarify your personal response:

  - What tone shifts can you discern in your oral reading of the passage? What do they reflect about your feelings? Are your feelings constant throughout or do they vary?

  - Do certain incidents or characters in the passage carry a particularly powerful emotional load? How do you respond to these incidents or characters?

  - What seems to be emotionally the most intense point in the passage?

  - What moments of ambivalent or mixed emotion do you find in the passage? What might be a reason for this uncertainty?

  - What is the emotional resolution of the passage (if one exists)?

  - What is your most prominent emotional response to the passage as a whole—anger, sorrow, joy, fear, vexation, disgust? Why?

Focal Judgments

For this journal assignment, you will make personal judgments about the most important words, passages, and aspects of the text. This activity was adapted from Milner and Milner (1993).

Procedure

- ◆ After reading a book, choose what you consider to be the most important word in the story. Give your rationale for the choice: why would it be most important?

♦ Return to the work and select the most important passage. Reduce the passage to a three- or four-word phrase that captures the entire story. Compare your phrase with the work's title to see if the two call up the same meaning. Reflect on the selected passage in terms of each of the following:

  • most important words

  • connection with total meaning

  • links with other passages

  • feeling, mood, tone

♦ Write what you consider the most important aspect of the story. Select, distill, and justify your choice.

♦ When you have selected your word, passage, and aspect, examine the three for connections. Answer the following questions:

  • Does the passage represent the aspect?

  • Does the word appear in the passage?

  • In what way are all three related to one another?

  • Does the work's title connect to all three?

Musical Response

Although English teachers have used music in many ways in the classroom, students can also have the opportunity to create music as a means of constructing meaning. Students can use their musical ability to compose tunes, lyrics, soundtracks, or find a theme song for a work of literature. A variation of this assignment is to ask students to find a song that expresses the themes and issues of the main character in a novel they are reading. For this journal response, ask students to choose one of the following options:

♦ Select a work of literature for which you would like to compose a rap, song, or soundtrack with the meaning interpreted through the lyrics, and the tone and mood illustrated through the music.

  • Set a poem to music or provide a musical background for the poem.

  • Compose a song that might serve as a "theme song."

  • Create a soundtrack for an oral interpretation of the novel.

  • Compose a rap interpreting a poem or theme in a novel.

♦ Perform your composition for the class, live or on videotape.

♦ Find a song that relates to the theme of your book or one for the main character. Explain the connections and associations you are making. Be sure to include a copy of the lyrics. If time permits to give an oral presentation, bring in a tape or CD and play a 30-second excerpt as you present your explanation

Assessment of Reader-Response Journals

For students to take journal writing seriously, they must receive feedback and evaluation. Otherwise, grade-conscious students will continue to treat them as unimportant or marginal to their coursework. You may want to respond to what students are saying with "reader-based" responses that describe ways you are "engaged, confused, intrigued, or puzzled by what students are saying" (Elbow, 1981; Johnston, 1983). Students can then experience how you are constructing meanings they are trying to convey. According to Anson and Beach, students are more likely to "prefer comments written in an informal, conversational mode, those that include self-disclosure, personal experiences or specific reactions" (1995, p. 180). Accordingly, written comments are more meaningful than using only an assessment rubric.

In my Young Adult literature course, there are three components to each Response Log assignment. First, students record the basic information: name, date, complete bibliographic information for the book (author, title, publishing information, ISBN number, genre, appropriate age/grade, interest level), brief summary of the plot, personal notes for ways to use the book with young adults, and evaluation of the book. Then, they complete a reader-response activity based on the multiple intelligences found on my Web site: http://www.dragonbbvs.com/members/18361. Third, students complete various analytical tasks which ask them to write a letter to a television or movie producer suggesting that the book be considered for a film, compare the book with the film/ video by the same title, or evaluate the book using various specified criteria. See *Reader-Response Log Assessment Rubric* on page 171.

Reader-Response Log Assessment Rubric

	Score of 4	Score of 3	Score of 2	Score of 1
Basic Information	Correct format; correct bibliographic information; informative summary; insightful personal notes; excellent evaluation	Mostly correct format; mostly correct bibliographic information; adequate summary; good personal notes; adequate evaluation	Errors in format; errors in bibliographic information; inadequate summary; inadequate personal notes, inadequate evaluation	Sketchy information about the book; lack of understanding in personal notes; inadequate or missing evaluation
Reader-Response Activity	Superior literary or visual appeal (layout, use of color and space); complete, original project including super explanation of the project (½ to ¾ page); textual support for main themes, purpose, characters, or events; personal connections made	Excellent literary or visual appeal (layout, use of color and space); complete, creative project including adequate explanation of the project; some textual support for the themes, purpose, characters or events; personal connections made	Good literary or visual appeal (layout, use of color and space); incomplete project and an inadequate or skimpy explanation of the project, little or no textual support for the themes, purposes, characters or events	Some attempt to do the project and brief explanation of it. Low-quality craftsmanship and no textual support for the project; no personal connections
Analytical Activity	Students make generalizations, inferences, reflections, judgments and evaluations of the text and literature they are reading	Students go beyond retelling to actively constructing meaning; excellent analytical skills; good interpretation	Students recount/retell what the text describes; explanation is stereotypical or ambiguous	Some attempt to complete the assignment, but response is inadequate

TOTAL (12 points for each journal entry):

Bibliography

Anson, C. M., & Beach, R. (1995). *Journals in the classroom: Writing to learn.* Norwood, MA: Christopher-Gordon.

Berger, L. R. (1996) Reader response journals: You make the meaning…and how. *Journal of Adolescent and Adult Literacy, 2,* 380–385.

Bleich, D. (1975). *Readings and feelings: An introduction to subjective criticism.* Urbana, IL: National Council of Teachers of English.

Elbow, P. (1981). *Writing with power.* New York: Oxford University Press.

Glasgow, J. (2001). *Utilizing multiple intelligences in reader response activities.* Available at: http://www.dragonbbs.com/members/18361.

Hancock, M. (March 1993). Exploring and extending personal response through literature journals. *Reading Teacher, 46,* 466–474.

Johnston, B. (1983). *Assessing English.* Urbana, IL: National Council of Teachers of English.

Kelly, P. R. (March 1990). Guiding young students' response to literature. *Reading Teacher, 43,* 474–470.

Kooy, M. (1993). *Responding to literature in the journal.* Paper presented at the Meeting of the National Conference on Reading, San Antonio, TX.

Milner, J., & Milner, L. (1993). *Bridging English.* NewYork: Maxwell Macmillan International.

Pritchard, J. R. (March 1993). Developing writing prompts for reading response and analysis. *English Journal, 82,* 24–32.

Rosenblatt, L. (1995). *Literature as exploration.* New York: Modern Language Association.

Rosenblatt, L. (1978). *The reader, the text, the poem: The transactional theory of the literary work.* Carbondale, IL: Southern Illinois University Press.

15

SKETCHBOOK JOURNAL

Janie Reinart

Pictures as well as words are important to human beings in their communication; we need to expand our narrow definition of literacy to include visual dimensions, and in so doing answer the call of researchers for the recognition of multi-literacies and ways these literacies can work to complement each other.

Ruth Hubbard

Overview of Authentic Learning

How do students learn to have fun with writing and develop the habits of a writer? Using a sketchbook journal, students will be writing and drawing on a daily basis. This self-graded project involves playing with words and collecting ideas for future writing. Grammar and spelling is not a concern in this type of informal writing. Students are encouraged to experiment by using color and graphics, integrating pictures with words, and finding a balance of art and writing. Students fill in weekly rubrics with detailed written support for their self-grade. A teacher-created rubric is available to guide students in various areas of assessment. Teachers should collect sketchbook journals biweekly, observe student's progress, and conference with students about their work. Students should be encouraged to journal in class as a reader-response activity or in response to a prompt, but they should also feel free to journal at home when they feel inspired to do so. Teacher modeling, by the teacher's keeping a journal, is highly recommended.

NCTE/IRA Standards

In this assessment, students will:

♦ Draw and write daily entries in a sketchbook. In doing so, students will adjust their use of spoken, written, and visual language to communicate effectively with a variety of audiences and for different purposes (NCTE/IRA Standard #3); they will employ a wide range of strategies as they write, and will use different writing process elements appropriately to communicate with different audiences for a variety of purposes (NCTE/IRA Standard #4); and, students whose first language is not English can make use of their first language to develop competency in the English language arts and to develop understanding of content across the curriculum (NCTE/IRA Standard #10).

♦ Collect words, phrases, and graphics from media resources. In doing so, students will apply knowledge of language structure, language conventions, media techniques, figurative language, and genre to create, critique, and discuss print and nonprint texts (NCTE/IRA Standard #6); they will conduct research on issues and interests by generating ideas and questions, and by posing problems. They will gather, evaluate, and synthesize data from a variety of sources to communicate their discoveries in ways that suit their purpose and audience (NCTE/IRA Standard #7); and, they will develop an understanding of, and respect for, diversity in language use, patterns, and dialects across cultures, ethnic groups, geographic regions, and social roles (NCTE/IRA Standard #8).

♦ Publish finished pieces that originated in the Sketchbook. In doing so, students will participate as knowledgeable, reflective, creative, and critical members of a variety of literacy communities (NCTE/IRA Standard #11), and they will use spoken, written, and visual language to accomplish their own purposes (NCTE/IRA Standard #12).

Materials

Students need:

♦ Any size artist sketchbook (wire-bound sketchbooks last longer)
♦ Assessment rubric
♦ Colored pencils
♦ Markers
♦ Magazine cutouts
♦ Glue or tape
♦ Photo

Performance Tasks

♦ Students will be writing on a daily basis in a notebook or writing folder that has provision for blank pages for drawing and lined paper for writing. This notebook is the source for creating ideas or "seeds" for growing into writing projects. Students should be encouraged to experiment with freewriting (writing nonstop for an extended period), associative writing, and other informal personal types of writing. The purpose is to encourage fluency and generate ideas, rather than focus on correct grammar and spelling in the notebook.

- In this special sketchbook, students should develop the habit of collecting thoughts, making short entries all through the day, recording memorable words and phrases, quotations, and news stories or articles, responding to literature, jotting down observations and overheard conversations, and drawing sketches of objects that catch the eye. They can also include photographs, song lyrics, or other artifacts that stimulate ideas or inspire them.

- It is from these selected sketches and pieces of writing that students will draft, share, revise, edit, and publish larger works. Here, they should have fun and experiment: play with colors and sizes; play with words. Students use the enclosed rubric to grade their own work and/or the work of others. Sketchbooks should be turned in biweekly.

- Regardless of the assessment decisions, students should be encouraged to share different entries during the week. Sometimes, all they need is an invitation. See *Assessment Rubric for Sketchbooks* on page 176.

Sample Assignments

- Using a photo or magazine cutout, ask students to glue a photo/ picture to the middle of page in journal and web words around picture. (See page 177 for *Illustrated Word Web*.) Use this brainstorming as a start for a story or poem. Using words cut from magazines or newspapers, have students create a found poem (See page 177 for *Found Poem*.)

- Make a memory map. Draw a map (floor plan) of the room you slept in at age four or five. Draw the map from a bird's eye view, looking down at the room. Fill at least half of a page with your floor plan and label the furniture, window, doorway, closet, etc. Now, writing in present tense as if you are four or five, begin describing your favorite toys, books, scary places, favorite clothing, hidden treasures, pets, pictures, music, games, etc. When you have recalled at least ten memories, begin crafting a poem from your memory map. For more ideas, see Dunning and Stafford (1992), *Getting the Knack: 20 Poetry Writing Exercises*.

Assessment Rubric for Sketchbooks

	Exemplary	*Acceptable*	*Not Yet*
Set-up: Organization	Evidence of daily entries with a balance of art/graphics and writing; colorful, neat; labels for date, time, title	At least three entries per week; fairly good balance of art and graphics with writing; good use of color; date, time, title are labeled; fairly neat	Entries are inconsistent and sparse; imbalance of art and writing; not so neat; need more color; missing labels for date, time, and titles of entries
Topics	Variety of topics addressed; elaborate responses; shows initiative, creativity and self-direction	Tends to write about the same topic; entries clearly communicate ideas through art and writing	The suggested topics are inadequately addressed; ideas are not clearly or fully communicated
Intensity	Evidence of insight and experimentation with graphics and text; personalizes the assignment; shares openly from past experiences and present situations	Shows commitment to the assignments. Not much experimentation with word play or artistic design. Entries tend to be objective, rather than subjective	Not much commitment to the sketchbook. Entries show a limited use of language and artistic appeal

Illustrated Word Web and Found Poem

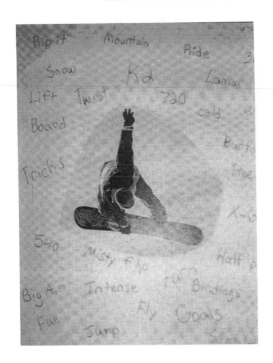 

Bibliography

Dunning, S., & Stafford, W. (1992). *Getting the knack: 20 poetry writing exercises*. Urbana, IL: National Council of Teachers of English.

REFERENCES

Anson, C. M., & Beach, R. (1995). *Journals in the classroom: Writing to learn.* Norwood, MA: Christopher-Gordon.

Asimov, I., & Pohl, F. (1991). *Our angry earth.* New York: Tom Doherty Associates.

Auden, W. H. (1945). *If I could tell you* [Online]. Available: http://recmusic.org/lieder/a/ audent/a1.html.

Beach, R. (1993). *A teacher's introduction to reader-response theories.* Urbana, IL: NCTE.

Berger, L. R. (1996) Reader response journals: You make the meaning… and how. *Journal of Adolescent and Adult Literacy, 2,* 380–385.

Bleich, D. (1975). *Readings and feelings: An introduction to subjective criticism.* Urbana, IL: National Council of Teachers of English.

Boston Pops Orchestra. John Williams. (1996) *O Fortuna.* On Summon the heroes [CD]. New York: Sony Classical.

Britton, J., Burgess, T., Martin, N., McLeod, A., & Rosen, H. (1977). *The development of writing abilities (11–18).* Hong Kong: Macmillan Education.

Claggett, F. *A measure of success: From assignment to assessment in English language arts.* Portsmouth, NH: Heinemann Boynton/Cook Publishers.

Corcoran, B. (Ed.). (1994). *Knowledge in the making.* Portsmouth, NH: Heinemann.

Daniels, H. (1994). *Literature circles: Voice and choice in the student-centered classroom.* York, ME: Stenhouse Publishers.

Daniels, H., & Bizar, M. (1998). *Methods that matter: Six structures for best practice classrooms.* York, ME: Stenhouse Publishers.

Dobson, A. (1987). In F. Mayes. *The discovery of poetry.* San Diego: Harcourt Brace Jovanovich.

Dunning, S., & Stafford, W. (1992). *Getting the knack: 20 poetry writing exercises.* Urbana, IL: National Council of Teachers of English.

Edelman, B. (1985). *Dear America: Letters home from Vietnam.* New York: Pocket Books, Simon & Schuster.

Elbow, P. (1981). *Writing with power.* New York: Oxford University Press.

Enya. (1988). *Exile.* On Watermark [CD]. Burbank, CA: Wea/Warner Brothers.

Farell, E. (1996). *Standards for the English language arts.* Urbana, IL: National Council of Teachers of English/International Reading Association.

Future Problem Solving Program, Inc. (2000). *FPSP Coach's Handbook.* Lexington, KY: Author.

Gardner, H. (1983). *Frames of mind: The theory of multiple intelligences.* New York: Basic Books.

Glasgow, J. (2001). *Utilizing multiple intelligences in reader response to activities* [Online]. Available : http://www.dragonbbs.com/members/1836/.

Glatthorn, A. A. (1999). *Performance standards authentic learning.* Larchmont, NY: Eye on Education.

Goldberg, N. (1990). *Wild mind.* New York: Bantam Books.

Hacker, M. (1980). In F. Mayes. *The discovery of poetry.* San Diego: Harcourt Brace Jovanovich.

Hancock, M. (2000). *A celebration of literature and response: Children, books, and teachers in K–8 classrooms.* Columbus, Ohio: Merrill, Prentice Hall.

Hancock, M. (March 1993). *Exploring and extending personal response through literature journals.* Reading Teacher, 46, 466–474.

Harling, R. (Director). (1999). *Evening star* [Film]. Starring Shirley MacClaine and Bill Paxton. Hollywood, CA: Paramount Studios.

Howes, B. (1959). In F. Mayes. *The discovery of poetry.* San Diego: Harcourt Brace Jovanovich.

Hughes, L. (1926). *Poems (to F.S.).* Alfred A. Knopf.

Johnston, B. (1983). *Assessing English.* Urbana, IL: National Council of Teachers of English.

Kelly, P. R. (March 1990). Guiding young students' response to literature. *Reading Teacher,* 43, 464–470.

Kilian, C. (April 2001). *Advice on novel writing* [Online]. Available: http://www.steampunk.com/sfch/writing/ckilian/.

Kiner, C. S., & Hume, K. C. (2000). *Future problem solving program: Evaluation primer.* Lexington, KY: Future Problem Solving Program, Inc.

Kooy, M. (1993). *Responding to literature in the journal.* Paper presented at the Meeting of the National Conference on Reading, San Antonio, TX.

Krisher, T. (1999). *Spite fences.* New York: Econo-Clad Books.

Lehmans non-electric catalogue. (1998). One Lehman Circle, P.O. Box 321, Kidron, OH 44646- 0321.

MacLeish, A. (1987). In F. Mayes. *The discovery of poetry.* San Diego: Harcourt Brace Jovanovich.

Macrorie, K. (1988). *The I-search paper: Revised edition of searching writing.* Portsmouth, NH: Boynton/Cook Publishers.

Making a personal brochure. (1992). Fort Collins, CO: Cottonwood Press.

Manhattan Transfer. (1990) *Capim. On Brasil* [CD]. New York: Atlantic.

Markel, M. H. (1992). *Technical writing: Situations and strategies.* New York: Martin's Press.

Marzano, R. J., & Kendall, J.S. (1996). *A comprehensive guide to designing standards-based districts, schools, and classrooms.* Alexandria, VA: Association for Supervision and Curriculum Development.

Mayes, F. (1987). *The discovery of poetry.* San Diego: Harcourt Brace Jovanovich.

Mehlich, S., & Smith-Worthington, D. (1997) *Technical writing for success: A school-to-work approach.* Cincinnati, OH: South-Western Educational Publishing.

Milner, J. O., & Milner, L.F.M. (1999). *Bridging English,* (2nd ed.). Upper Saddle River, New Jersey: Prentice Hall.

Moffett, J. (1981). *Active voice: A writing program across the curriculum.* Upper Montclair, NJ: Boynton/Cook Publishers.

Myers, M., & Spalding, E. (1997). *Standards exemplar series: Assessing student performance grades 9–12.* Urbana, IL: National Council of Teachers of English.

Myers, W. D. (1988). *Fallen angels.* New York: Scholastic.

O'Brien, R. (1987). *Z for Zachariah.* New York: Aladdin Paperbacks.

Ohio Department of Education. (2001). *High school proficiency testing: Fact sheets.*

Olson, C., & Schiesl, S. A multiple intelligences approach to teaching multicultural literature. *Language Arts Journal of Michigan,* 1, 12, 21–28.

Orr, D. W. (1994). *Earth in mind: On education, environment, and the human prospect.* Washington, DC: Island Press.

Pearce, R. (Director). (1997). *The long walk home* [Film]. Starring Sissy Spacek and Whoopi Goldberg. Artisan Entertainment.

Pickett, N., & Dodge, B. (June 20, 2001). *Rubrics for Web lessons* [Online]. Available: http://edweb.sdsu.edu/webquest/rubrics/welessons.htm.

Powell, D. (1981). *What can I write about? 7000 topics for high school students.* Urbana, IL: National Council of Teachers of English.

Pritchard, J. R. (March 1993). Developing writing prompts for reading response and analysis. *English Journal,* 82, 24–32.

Rexroth, K. *One hundred poems from the Japanese.* New York: New Directions.

Ritt, M. (Director). (1979). *Norma Rae* [VHS]. Starring Sally Field.

Rosenblatt, L. (1995). *Literature as exploration.* New York: Modern Language Association.

Rosenblatt, L. (1978). *The reader, the text, the poem: The transactional theory of the literary work.* Carbondale, IL: Southern Illinois University Press.

Seethaler, S. (Spring 2000). *SCOPE: Genetically Modified Foods in Perspective* [Online]. Available: http://wise.berkeley.edu/teacher/projects/lessonPlan.php?id=14.

Shelton, R. (Director). (2001). *Tin cup* [Film]. Starring Kevin Costner and Rene Russo. Burbank, CA: Warner Studios.

Standards for the English language arts. (1996). Urbana, IL: National Council of Teachers of English/International Reading Association.

Starr, L. (2000). *A good rubric.* Education World.

Stiggins, R. J. (1997). *Student-centered classroom assessment* (2nd ed.). Columbus, OH: Merrill.

Streisand, Barbara (Director). (2001). *The mirror has two faces* [Film]. Starring Barbara Streisand and Jeff Bridges. Culver City, CA: Columbia/Tristar.

Voigt,C. (1995). *Izzy, Willy, Nilly.* New York: Alladdin Paperbooks.

Witt, H. (1987). In F. Mayes. *The discovery of poetry.* San Diego: Harcourt Brace Jovanovich.

Wolff, V. E. (1993). *Make lemonade.* New York: Henry Holt and Co.